ADVANCED PROGRAMMING
IN MICROSOFT BASIC

ADVANCED PROGRAMMING IN MICROSOFT BASIC

Gabriel Cuéllar

A Reston Computer Group Book

Reston Publishing Company, Inc.
A Prentice-Hall Company
Reston, Virginia

Library of Congress Cataloging in Publication Data
Cuéllar, Gabriel.
    Advanced programming in microsoft Basic.

    1. Basic (Computer program language) I. Title.
QA76.73.B3C8   1983   001.64'24   84–13710
ISBN 0–8359–0059–2

Copyright 1984 by
Reston Publishing Company, Inc.
A Prentice-Hall Company
11480 Sunset Hills Road
Reston, Virginia 22090

10   9   8   7   6   5   4   3   2   1

Printed in the United States of America

To my wife Mila.

CONTENTS

ACKNOWLEDGMENTS

I would like to thank Rodolfo LaRota, Paulo Laserna, Guillermo Türk, Lee Cooprider, Ellis Horowitz, Mario and Susana Correa, Bob Howland, my parents, brothers and sister.

INTRODUCTION

This book is intended for those who are already familiar with Microsoft's BASIC-80 and want to write more "professional" programs with it. It is basically a collection of methods and techniques to let you do things that would otherwise be slow, impractical, or even impossible.

We use both of the terms BASIC and BASIC-80 to refer to Microsoft's BASIC-80 versions 5.0 or higher. Every single program line in the book is written in BASIC. There is no use of machine-language routines at all.

The first chapter, *Input*, teaches you how to gain control over the input in a number of ways. You might say, "But I have never lost control!" Well, maybe you as a programmer have not, because you know how things operate and never do what you are not supposed to, but when your program is run by a person who does not know (and does not *want* to know) the internal operation of the program, the input is the part where most things can go wrong.

In Chapter 2, *Output*, we study some techniques to complement the formatting capabilities of PRINT USING, as well as methods to accelerate the creation of screens.

Chapter 3 deals with one of the headaches of programming: *Handling Data*. We study a number of sorting techniques, both for data in memory and for data on disk, as well as methods to search, delete, insert, and modify efficiently your collections of data.

In Chapter 4, *Files*, we study some ways to handle access to disk efficiently.

Chapter 5, *Functions*, introduces a very powerful concept that has not been fully exploited. We study some commonly needed functions, Boolean functions, how to create functions that make decisions between two or more options, and how to work with nonstandard data types. All this will allow you to define and debug functions that can later be used as if they were part of the language.

Chapter 6, *Pointers*, introduces another powerful concept that will let you use subroutines with local variables as if they were functions. With this concept, you will be able to make a numeric variable store a value of a different type, to make two variables share the same area in memory, to store arrays of numbers in strings or strings in arrays of numbers, and to move entire arrays with very few instructions.

In Chapter 7, *Utilities*, we examine binary numbers and Boolean values, two commonly used concepts in computers. We also look at a useful program that will be explained at the end of this introduction.

It is the author's firm belief that if you use the techniques shown in this book, your programs will be more efficient, more professional looking, and much easier to create and maintain.

STRUCTURED PROGRAMMING

Structured programming has gained such wide acceptance, that most modern computer languages deliberately make it difficult to write programs in a nonstructured way.

The idea behind structured programming is to break big problems into smaller parts that can be independently solved and analyzed; these smaller parts are broken into yet smaller ones, and so forth, until what is left is essentially a problem in how to code in the basic instruction of the language. Structured programming facilitates the study of each of the subtasks we have to perform; we as humans cannot cope with processes that are too complicated, often losing sight of the forest for the trees.

The first versions of BASIC offered very few tools for structured programming: the only looping structure was the FOR loop, and the IF .. THEN did not include an ELSE part, forcing painfully frequent GOTO's. Microsoft's BASIC-80 is the most extensive implementation of BASIC available for microcomputers. Very powerful and easy to program, it has some of the tools necessary to write programs in a way that comes close to structured programming.

Let's see what structured programming in BASIC-80 is all about. Program Fragment 0.1 shows a primitive way to write a program.

```
500 W$=INPUT$(1)
510 IF W$<>CHR$(13) THEN 540
520 IF COUNTER<10 THEN PRINT"Insufficient chararacters ":GOTO 500
530 RETURN
540 PRINT W$;:COUNTER=COUNTER+1:GOTO 500
```

Program Fragment 0.1 Unstructured IF . . THEN

Notice how difficult it is to understand what even such a small program as this does. Because of the GOTO's (or the THEN followed by a line number, which is the same thing), we have to leave a part of the program behind for later analysis while we go somewhere else to see why we are sent there. Compare the modern version shown in Program Fragment 0.2.

```
500 W$=INPUT$(1)
510 IF W$=CHR$(13)
        THEN
           IF COUNTER<10
             THEN
                PRINT"Insufficient characters"
             ELSE
                RETURN
        ELSE
           PRINT W$;:COUNTER=COUNTER+1
520 GOTO 500
```

Program Fragment 0.2 Structured IF . . THEN . . ELSE

The first difference is that the ELSE part of the comparison has been included. This takes away at least one GOTO per IF instruction. Since nested IF's are allowed, the corresponding THEN . . ELSE's have been indented. This facilitates the identification of the different parts of the nesting.

It might seem that there are instructions without line numbers. However, these are really subinstructions of a larger instruction which bears the line number. The introduction of special characters allows this "ghost line" positioning. Those characters are:

Space: Any number of spaces can be added between instructions, as long as they do not split a command in two. The following two lines are equivalent:

$$10 \ X = (3^*E - (12/SIN(E^2)))$$
$$10 \ X = (3 * E - (12 / SIN(E \ 2))),$$

But these are not:

$$10 \ PRINT \ 123$$
$$10 \ PRI \ NT \ 123.$$

Line-Feed: Produced by Ctrl-J, the line-feed sends the cursor to the left margin of the next line. As with the space, any number of line-feeds between instructions is totally ignored by BASIC.

Tab: Produced by Ctrl-I (if your terminal does not have a TAB key), the tab sends the cursor to the next tab position. Beginning at the left margin, tabs are placed every eight columns.

With these three characters, you can achieve any kind of indentation, as shown in Program Fragment 0.2.

Indentation helps visualize structures that are logically separated, such as the internal part of a FOR loop. (See Program Fragment 0.3.)

```
10 FOR I=1 TO 100:
        S=I*2:PRINT I,S:
        IF S=50
           THEN
               PRINT"Halfway !"
20 NEXT
```

Program Fragment 0.3

Any group of instructions that are nested should be indented to clearly indicate the different levels of nesting. Here is a version of Program Fragment 0.2 showing nesting without indentation. Comparing Program Fragment 0.4 with 0.2, this version seems cryptic!

```
10 IF W=1 THEN PRINT"First number is "M(1) ELSE IF M(W)>10 THEN
PRINT"Greater than ten" ELSE PRINT"Forget about it."
20 W=W+1:GOTO 10
```

Program Fragment 0.4

WHILE loops are another powerful tool in structured programming. Testing for the truth of a comparison, they allow completely different constructions than those of the FOR loop. Program Fragment 0.5 reads a file of unknown length:

```
10 IF EOF(1)
       THEN
           20
       ELSE
           INPUT#1,M(I):I=I+1:GOTO 10
20 CLOSE
```

Program Fragment 0.5

Program Fragment 0.6 is the same program with a WHILE loop:

```
10 WHILE NOT EOF(1):
      INPUT#1,M(I):I=I+1:
   WEND:CLOSE
```

Program Fragment 0.6

Another way of making your programs understandable is to use variable names that clearly indicate their purpose. Names such as I and J are fine for temporary counters, but whenever a variable serves a specific purpose, its name should reflect it. BASIC recognizes distinct variables of up to forty characters, i.e., letters or numbers. An additional convenience is the decimal point, which can be used anywhere in the variable except as its first character, which must always be a letter. Here are examples of valid variable names:

NAME$

NICK.NAME$

POSITION%

NEW.POSITION

The use of the special characters to indent your program has a small effect on the performance of the program. This effect is always so small, that it can hardly be measured, and the time saved in programming and debugging is well worth the delay. However, if you need those extra milliseconds or the space taken by those characters, Chapter 7 shows a way to return a program to its original unstructured form.

INPUT

1

The usual way to do input from the keyboard is by means of the INPUT and LINE INPUT commands. Unfortunately, when these commands are executed, the program loses control until a ⟨return⟩ signals the end of the input. During the time control is lost, many unwanted things can happen. Here is a list of some of them:

1. The program stops until RETURN signals the end of the input; therefore, the computer cannot perform any other function but wait.

2. Any number of characters can be typed, from zero to 255. Anything typed when this maximum is reached, except for the backspace, the Ctrl-X, and the ⟨return⟩, is ignored.

3. If the variable used in the input is of numeric type, a string will cause a 'redo from start' to the PRINTed and the INPUT repeated. LINE INPUT cannot be used with a numeric variable.

4. If a number is expected, and an OVERFLOW condition occurs (i.e., more digits are typed than the variable can take), 'redo from start' will make the program repeat the input.

5. If Ctrl-X is typed, the line of input is canceled, a ''#'' is printed, and the cursor jumps to the next line. If the cursor was in the bottom line, the entire screen is scrolled.

6. The following are examples of strings that are accepted as 0 in a numeric variable: ., + − − − − − − + ., .E, .D, .E2, .D − 12.

7. One single tab (Ctrl-I) can send the cursor to up to eight positions to the right, sometimes disturbing and even destroying the contents of the screen.

The following apply only to INPUT (not to LINE INPUT):

8. If a comma is included in the characters typed, the characters following it will be ignored, and the error message 'redo from start' will be PRINTed.

9. If a double set of quotes is used, the 'redo from start' error message will be printed.

10. If quotes are used, they will not be included in the string.

11. Ctrl-O, Ctrl-S, and Ctrl-U have the effects described in the standard BASIC-80 manuals. Since these commands are controlled by the operating system (the program that controls BASIC) or by BASIC itself, they cannot be detected by a program at this level. The only way to avoid their action is to redefine these characters via the CONFIGIO command (if you are under CP/M; see the corresponding manual for details on how to redefine characters) or some equivalent instruction.

The goal of this chapter is to present ways to gain control over the above situations.

1.1 REJECTING UNWANTED CHARACTERS

The first thing that must be done to control the input is to reject control characters or sequences of control characters that either might produce undesirable results on the display or might generate special effects peculiar to particular terminals. Toward this end, program REJECT simulates the INPUT command, with the advantage that it completely ignores those unwanted characters.

In REJECT, a single character is read from the keyboard, using the INPUT$(1) function. (When used with 1 as argument, INPUT$ returns every character typed without waiting for a ⟨return⟩.) The character is analyzed, and only those in the range " " .. CHR$(127), which includes every printable character,[1] are accepted. (In a later section, we will study some further useful restrictions of this range.) If W$ is outside the range, line 1030 goes to line 1010 to fetch a new character.

---

[1]Chr$(127) was used instead of the variable with the last character because it is easier to remember that there are only 127 standard ASCII codes.

When the character is a legal one, it is echoed (printed on the screen) and added to BUFF$, which stores every character accepted.

```
10 '
                        ** REJECT **
                   Reject control characters.

20 CTRL.H$=CHR$(8):CR.RET$=CHR$(13):
     BKSPC$=CTRL.H$+" "+CTRL.H$
30 PRINT"Type your name : ";:GOSUB 1000:
     NAM$=BUFF$:PRINT:PRINT NAM$:
     END

1000 BUFF$=""
1010 W$=INPUT$(1):
     IF W$>=" "AND W$<=CHR$(127)
          THEN 1050
1020 IF W$=CTRL.H$
     THEN
          IF BUFF$=""
          THEN
               1010
          ELSE
               BUFF$=LEFT$(BUFF$,LEN(BUFF$)-1):
               PRINT BKSPC$;:GOTO 1010
1030 IF W$=CR.RET$
     THEN
          RETURN
     ELSE
          1010
1050 PRINT W$;:BUFF$=BUFF$+W$:GOTO 1010
```

Program 1.1

Besides those in the range " " .. CHR$(127), there are two non-printable characters that must be accepted to simulate the most basic features of the input command: the left arrow (Ctrl-H) to correct mistakes, and ⟨return⟩ to signal the end of the input.

If Ctrl-H (CHR$(8) or backspace) is pressed, the previous character typed (if any), as well as the rightmost character of BUFF$, must be deleted. The easiest way to delete the character to the left of the cursor is to print a Ctrl-H, which moves the cursor to the previous position on the screen, follow it by a space to delete the character under the cursor, and finally print another Ctrl-H to leave the cursor in the empty spot. Instead of using three print statements and CHR$(8) to produce the Ctrl-H, the three characters can be assigned to a string variable. In program REJECT, this string has been called BKSPC$.

When line 1020 detects a Ctrl-H, it has to treat two cases:

1. If BUFF$ is empty, there is nothing to do, since there are no characters to erase.

2. If BUFF$ is not empty, the rightmost character must be deleted from the screen and from BUFF$.

Notice that the use of instruction 2 for the case of the empty BUFF$ would result in an error, since trying to evaluate LEFT$(BUFF$,LEN(BUFF$) − 1) when LEN(BUFF$) − 1 is a negative number, is illegal.

If the character typed is a carriage return (CHR$(13) or Ctrl-M), it is interpreted as the end of the input, and in line 1030 there is a subroutine RETURN. The characters that were accepted are now contained in BUFF$ and can be copied into the variable chosen for later use. Notice that the carriage return is not included in BUFF$.

Subroutine 1000 simulates the INPUT command with the convenient rejection of control characters. As a side effect, the problems of quotes, commas, and colons are eliminated: the input subroutine actually behaves like a LINE INPUT.

1.2 CONTROLLING THE LENGTH

Another problem with the INPUT statement is that it is impossible to specify the length of the input field: from zero to 255 characters can be typed. When the limit of 255 characters is reached, the bell character (which produces an audible beep in the terminal—however, not all terminals support this feature) is printed, and the additional characters are ignored. When more characters than expected are typed, parts of the display might be destroyed.

Program LENSTOP is a copy of program REJECT, with the addition of line 1050 that when a legal character is found (that is, it is printable), the length of BUFF$ is checked. If BUFF$ has as many characters as specified in INLEN% (a variable was chosen instead of a constant to give more flexibility to the input subroutine), the character is ignored; otherwise, the character is echoed and added to BUFF$. This way, when the desired length is reached, the input subroutine stops accepting characters, and there is no way to get outside of a specified field, thereby protecting screen displays.

```
10
                    ** LENSTOP **
                  control the length

20 CTRL.H$=CHR$(8):CR.RET$=CHR$(13):
   BKSPC$=CTRL.H$+" "+CTRL.H$
30 PRINT"Type your name : ";:INLEN%=20:GOSUB 1000:
   NAM$=BUFF$:PRINT:PRINT NAM$:
   END
```

```
1000 BUFF$=""
1010 W$=INPUT$(1):
        IF W$>=" "AND W$<=CHR$(127)
           THEN 1050
1020 IF W$=CTRL.H$
        THEN
            IF BUFF$=""
              THEN
                 1010
              ELSE
                 BUFF$=LEFT$(BUFF$,LEN(BUFF$)-1):
                 PRINT BKSPC$;:GOTO 1010
1030 IF W$=CR.RET$
        THEN
           RETURN
        ELSE
           1010
1050 IF LEN(BUFF$)=INLEN%
        THEN
           1010
        ELSE
           PRINT W$;:BUFF$=BUFF$+W$:GOTO 1010
```

Program 1.2

1.3 CONTINUING WHEN THE LENGTH IS REACHED

Many times the response to an input can be considered to be terminated when a certain length is reached. For example, in the input of a Y/N (yes or no) question, when either a "Y" or an "N" is typed, there is no need to wait for a ⟨return⟩ or any other character. Another example can be the input of the name of a day of the week, where the first two or three letters of the name are sufficient to produce an unambiguous answer.

In program LENCONT, since the number of characters that have been accepted can be checked at all times, when a character is accepted and added to BUFF$, line 1050 compares the resulting length with INLEN%. If BUFF$ has fewer characters than are needed to produce an unambiguous answer, the process is repeated; otherwise, the subroutine is terminated. This is equivalent to having an automatic ⟨return⟩.

Notice that the ⟨return⟩ can still be used in the usual way.

```
10 '
               ** LENCONT **
         Continue when length is reached

20 CTRL.H$=CHR$(8):CR.RET$=CHR$(13):
   BKSPC$=CTRL.H$+" "+CTRL.H$
```

```
30 PRINT"Type the date (MM/DD/YY) ";:
   INLEN%=2:GOSUB 1000:MONTH$=BUFF$:PRINT"/";:
   GOSUB 1000:DAY$=BUFF$:PRINT"/";:
   GOSUB 1000:YEAR$=BUFF$
40 PRINT:PRINT:
   PRINT"Date : ";MONTH$;"/";DAY$;"/";YEAR$:
   END

1000 BUFF$=""
1010 W$=INPUT$(1):
     IF W$>=" "AND W$<=CHR$(127)
         THEN 1050
1020 IF W$=CTRL.H$
         THEN
            IF BUFF$=""
               THEN
                  1010
               ELSE
                  BUFF$=LEFT$(BUFF$,LEN(BUFF$)-1):
                  PRINT BKSPC$;:GOTO 1010
1030 IF W$=CR.RET$
         THEN
            RETURN
         ELSE
            1010
1050 PRINT W$;:BUFF$=BUFF$+W$:
     IF LEN(BUFF$)=INLEN%
         THEN
            RETURN
         ELSE
            1010
```

Program 1.3

1.4 NUMERIC INPUT

In this section we will deal with the input of positive integers only. For floating-point and signed numbers, see Sections 1.14 and 1.17.

When you are using the input subroutine to fetch a number, it is a good idea to reject not only control characters, but letters and symbols too. Now that we are controlling every character entering through the keyboard, we can accept only those in the range ''0'' through ''9'', as shown in program INPNUMB. However, since everything other than numbers is being rejected (except for Ctrl-H, and ⟨return⟩), neither a decimal point nor a negative or positive sign can be entered.

```
10 '
                    ** INPNUMB **
                    Only numbers

20 CTRL.H$=CHR$(8):CR.RET$=CHR$(13):
   BKSPC$=CTRL.H$+" "+CTRL.H$
30 PRINT"Type your telephone number: ";:INLEN%=7:
   GOSUB 1000:TEL$=BUFF$:PRINT:
   PRINT"Telephone : ";TEL$:
   END

1000 BUFF$=""
1010 W$=INPUT$(1):
     IF W$>="0"AND W$<="9"
        THEN
           1050
1020 IF W$=CTRL.H$
        THEN
          IF BUFF$=""
            THEN
               1010
            ELSE
               BUFF$=LEFT$(BUFF$,LEN(BUFF$)-1):
               PRINT BKSPC$;:GOTO 1010
1030 IF W$=CR.RET$
        THEN
           RETURN
        ELSE
           1010
1050 IF LEN(BUFF$)=INLEN%
        THEN
           1010
        ELSE
           PRINT W$;:BUFF$=BUFF$+W$:GOTO 1010
```

Program 1.4

1.5 DELETING THE INPUT LINE

It is very convenient, especially when entering long lines, to have an option to erase the entire line with a single keystroke instead of backspacing many times. When Ctrl-X is typed while an INPUT command is being executed in BASIC, the characters previously typed are ignored, a "#" is printed, and the cursor jumps to the following line to allow the start of a new input. We will use the same character to delete the line, but in a more elegant way. When Ctrl-X is detected in line

1040 of program DELLINE, a number of BCKSPC$'s equal to the length of BUFF$ will be printed, deleting the entire field. (If BUFF$ is empty, the FOR loop will not be executed). Now that the screen has been updated, BUFF$ is emptied. Notice that Ctrl-H is still active for deletion of single characters.

```
10 '
                        ** DELLINE **
                  delete line

20 CTRL.H$=CHR$(8):CR.RET$=CHR$(13):
   BKSPC$=CTRL.H$+" "+CTRL.H$:CTRL.X$=CHR$(24)
30 PRINT"Type your name : ";:INLEN%=20:
   GOSUB 1000:NAM$=BUFF$:PRINT:PRINT NAM$:
   END

1000 BUFF$=""
1010 W$=INPUT$(1):
     IF W$>=" "AND W$<=CHR$(127)
        THEN
           1060
1020 IF W$=CTRL.H$
        THEN
           IF BUFF$=""
              THEN
                 1010
              ELSE
                 BUFF$=LEFT$(BUFF$,LEN(BUFF$)-1):
                 PRINT BKSPC$;:GOTO 1010
1030 IF W$=CR.RET$
        THEN
           RETURN
1040 IF W$=CTRL.X$
        THEN
           FOR I=1 TO LEN(BUFF$):
              PRINT BKSPC$;:
           NEXT:GOTO 1000
        ELSE
           1010
1060 IF LEN(BUFF$)=INLEN%
        THEN
           1010
        ELSE
           PRINT W$;:BUFF$=BUFF$+W$:GOTO 1010
```

Program 1.5

1.6 RESTORING THE DELETED LINE

The price to pay for the convenience of the delete-line key is that a mistake might make you lose a line. A useful option to add, then, is the restoration of the deleted line with a single key, saving unnecessary retyping.

In line 1040 of program RSTRLINE, the contents of the field are copied into ERASE.BUFF$ before deleting them when Ctrl-X is pressed. If Ctrl-R is detected in line 1050 (Ctrl-R is the command to restore the input line), the characters that may have been typed after the deletion must be erased, so that the restored line looks exactly the way it was when it was deleted. This is accomplished by printing as many BCKSPC$'s as there are characters in BUFF$. Then, ERASE.BUFF$ is printed and copied into BUFF$.

Notice that on entry to the input subroutine, ERASE.BUFF$ must be emptied, or else a Ctrl-R might restore a string deleted in a previous input field, perhaps conflicting with the length and type of this new field.

```
10                          ** RSTRLINE **
                         Restore line

20  CTRL.H$=CHR$(8):CR.RET$=CHR$(13):
    BKSPC$=CTRL.H$+" "+CTRL.H$:CTRL.R$=CHR$(18):
    CTRL.X$=CHR$(24)
30  PRINT"Type your name : ";:INLEN%=20:
    GOSUB 1000:NAM$=BUFF$:PRINT:PRINT NAM$:
    END

1000 ERASE.BUFF$=""
1005 BUFF$=""
1010 W$=INPUT$(1):
     IF W$>=" "AND W$<=CHR$(127)
         THEN
            1070
1020 IF W$=CTRL.H$
         THEN
            IF BUFF$=""
              THEN
                 1010
              ELSE
                 BUFF$=LEFT$(BUFF$,LEN(BUFF$)-1):
                 PRINT BKSPC$;:GOTO 1010
1030 IF W$=CR.RET$
         THEN
            RETURN
1040 IF W$=CTRL.X$
         THEN
            ERASE.BUFF$=BUFF$:
            FOR I=1 TO LEN(BUFF$):
              PRINT BKSPC$;:
            NEXT:GOTO 1005
1050 IF W$=CTRL.R$
         THEN
            FOR I=1 TO LEN(BUFF$):
```

```
        PRINT BKSPC$;:
     NEXT:
     BUFF$=ERASE.BUFF$:PRINT BUFF$;:GOTO 1010
1060 GOTO 1010
1070 IF LEN(BUFF$)=INLEN%
     THEN
        1010
     ELSE
        PRINT W$;:BUFF$=BUFF$+W$:GOTO 1010
```

Program 1.6

1.7 ADDING A PROMPT LINE

When the program expects some input, it is convenient not only to control the number of characters that are to be accepted, but to inform the user about the maximum length allowed before he actually 'crashes' against the right margin of the field. This can easily be done by printing a line of the same size as the input field. Underscores (CHR$(95), for those whose terminals do not have a key to produce them) and dots are commonly used, because they do not conflict visually with the other characters of the field, and therefore clearly indicate its length. This line must be printed on entry to the input subroutine before accepting any character. In line 1000 of program PROMPTLN, a STRING$(INLEN%,UNDRLN$) prints the line, and a STRING$(INLEN%,CTRL.H$) returns the cursor to the beginning of the line. From that moment on, every character accepted and echoed will replace one underline. When Ctrl-H is used to delete one character, the BCKSPC$ described in Section 1.1 cannot be used because it deletes the character to the left of the cursor and replaces it by a space. In this particular case, we want to replace it with an underline. BCKSPC$ is therefore constructed with a Ctrl-H, an underline, and another Ctrl-H.

When the subroutine RETURNs, line 1030 erases the underlines that remain in the field by printing a number of spaces. Other than that, the procedure is the same as in the previous input subroutines.

```
10 '
                ** PROMPTLN **
                Prompt line

20 CTRL.H$=CHR$(8):CR.RET$=CHR$(13):
   UNDRLN$=CHR$(95):CTRL.R$=CHR$(18):
   BKSPC$=CTRL.H$+UNDRLN$+CTRL.H$:CTRL.X$=CHR$(24)
30 PRINT"Type your name : ";:INLEN%=20:GOSUB 1000:
   NAM$=BUFF$:PRINT:PRINT NAM$:
   END
```

```
1000 ERASE.BUFF$=""
1005 BUFF$="":PRINT STRING$(INLEN%,UNDRLN$);
                    STRING$(INLEN%,CTRL.H$);
1010 W$=INPUT$(1):
     IF W$>=" "AND W$<=CHR$(127)
        THEN
           1070
1020 IF W$=CTRL.H$
        THEN
           IF BUFF$=""
              THEN
                 1010
              ELSE
                 BUFF$=LEFT$(BUFF$,LEN(BUFF$)-1):
                 PRINT BKSPC$;:GOTO 1010
1030 IF W$=CR.RET$
        THEN
           PRINT STRING$(INLEN%-LEN(BUFF$)," ");:
           RETURN
1040 IF W$=CTRL.X$
        THEN
           ERASE.BUFF$=BUFF$:
           FOR I=1 TO LEN(BUFF$):
             PRINT BKSPC$;:
           NEXT:GOTO 1005
1050 IF W$=CTRL.R$
        THEN
           FOR I=1 TO LEN(BUFF$):
             PRINT BKSPC$;:
           NEXT:
           BUFF$=ERASE.BUFF$:PRINT BUFF$;:GOTO 1010
1060 GOTO 1010
1070 IF LEN(BUFF$)=INLEN%
        THEN
           1010
        ELSE
           PRINT W$;:BUFF$=BUFF$+W$:GOTO 1010
```

Program 1.7

1.8 DEFAULT VALUES

When many items of the same or a similar kind must be input into a program, it is often the case that there are values or strings that are common to several entries, and yet they must be retyped every time. Consider the case of a company that processes many receipts daily: the individual lines entered will have repetitions of the same date, same receipt number, etc. Even worse is the situation in which an input field has the same value most of the time, except for the few cases in which it varies. An elegant way to handle this is to allow regular input, but to provide the answer to the input when an empty string is typed—that is, if ⟨return⟩ is pressed when the input field is empty. In the example of the receipts, when the date is the same as in the previous line, a ⟨return⟩ will suffice to have the date typed for you and assigned to BUFF$, whereupon the input will be terminated on RETURNing from the subroutine.

In program DEFAULT, line 25 assigns values to both of the variables REC and YEAR, and line 30 calls the input subroutine, sending to the variable DEFLT$ the string to assign to BUFF$ as default. When the loop is repeated, the value taken will be the previous one chosen, not necessarily the one assigned in line 25. The excess underlines are deleted in line 1035, and if BUFF$ is found empty, DEFLT$ is printed and copied into BUFF$ before returning from the subroutine.

```
10  '
                        ** DEFAULT **
                          Default

20  CTRL.H$=CHR$(8):CR.RET$=CHR$(13):
    UNDRLN$=CHR$(95):CTRL.R$=CHR$(18):
    BKSPC$=CTRL.H$+UNDRLN$+CTRL.H$:CTRL.X$=CHR$(24)
25  REC#=12345:YEAR=1983
30  PRINT"Receipt number : ";:INLEN%=10:
    DEFLT$=STR$(REC#):GOSUB 1000:
    PRINT:REC#=VAL(BUFF$):
    PRINT"Year : ";:INLEN%=4:DEFLT$=STR$(YEAR):
    GOSUB 1000:PRINT:YEAR=VAL(BUFF$):GOTO 30
40  PRINT:PRINT"Receipt : "REC$:
    PRINT"Year     : "YEAR$:
    END

1000 ERASE.BUFF$=""
1005 BUFF$="":
     PRINT STRING$(INLEN%,UNDRLN$);
           STRING$(INLEN%,CTRL.H$);
1010 W$=INPUT$(1):
     IF W$>=" "AND W$<=CHR$(127)
        THEN
           1070
1020 IF W$=CTRL.H$
        THEN
           IF BUFF$=""
              THEN
                 1010
              ELSE
                 BUFF$=LEFT$(BUFF$,LEN(BUFF$)-1):
                 PRINT BKSPC$;:GOTO 1010
1030 IF W$<>CR.RET$
        THEN
           1040
        ELSE
```

```
1035     PRINT STRING$(INLEN%-LEN(BUFF$)," ");:
         IF BUFF$=""
            THEN
               BUFF$=DEFLT$:
               FOR I=1 TO INLEN%+1:
                 PRINT CTRL.H$;:
               NEXT:PRINT BUFF$;:RETURN
            ELSE
               RETURN
1040 IF W$=CTRL.X$
        THEN
           ERASE.BUFF$=BUFF$:
           FOR I=1 TO LEN(BUFF$):
             PRINT BKSPC$;:
           NEXT:GOTO 1005
1050 IF W$=CTRL.R$
        THEN
           FOR I=1 TO LEN(BUFF$):
             PRINT BKSPC$;:
           NEXT:
           BUFF$=ERASE.BUFF$:PRINT BUFF$;:GOTO 1010
1060 GOTO 1010
1070 IF LEN(BUFF$)=INLEN%
        THEN
           1010
        ELSE
           PRINT W$;:BUFF$=BUFF$+W$:GOTO 1010
```

Program 1.8

1.9 RETURNING TO THE MENU

One of the most popular ways to guide the user through a program is the MENU. Akin to the menu of a restaurant, a program MENU displays the different options preceded by some letter or number to facilitate the choice. When one of those numbers or letters is pressed, execution continues in the corresponding part of the program. But equally important as allowing the choice of which part of the program is to execute is to have a way to change your mind and return to the menu from anywhere in the program.

One way to do this would be to display a message every once in a while asking the user to type a code if he wants to return to the menu or to press any other key to continue. Easy as this is to implement, however, it would become tedious and would delay the execution of the program.

A better way is to choose a key which, if pressed during an input, will make the program return to the menu. In program MENURET, ⟨esc⟩ (ESCAPE or CHR$(27)) was chosen as such a key. Its action will be similar to a ⟨return⟩, but instead of returning from the subroutine, it will return to the menu. Since this implies aborting the input, it is a good idea to erase the entire line, both the characters typed and the additional underlines that may remain to the right of the field.

The entry to the input subroutine was accomplished through a subroutine call, and the exit will be done with a GOTO (to go to the menu). Therefore, the POP command must be used. When a subroutine is called, the address to return to when the corresponding RETURN is found is stored. If a new subroutine call takes place before the first one has RETURNed, the new address is stored too, and the process can be repeated a number of times. These addresses are stored in such a way that the RETURN is done in the reverse order in which the subroutines were called: the last one entered is the first one used. The place where these addresses are stored is called the stack and has a limited size. If the exit of the input subroutine is done with a GOTO when the ⟨esc⟩ jumps back to the menu, the address of the subroutine will remain stored. If many calls to the subroutine are made, there is a chance that the stack will run out of space. POP clears one return address from the stack.

If your BASIC does not have the POP command, an alternative solution is to have a variable that is set to TRUE (see Boolean variables, Section 7.2) when the RETURN from the subroutine is caused by an ⟨esc⟩ rather than by a ⟨return⟩. On return from the input subroutine, the variable is tested, and the program jumps to the menu if the variable is found to be TRUE.

```
10 '
                        ** MENURET **
                        Return to menu

20 CTRL.H$=CHR$(8):CR.RET$=CHR$(13):
   UNDRLN$=CHR$(95):CTRL.R$=CHR$(18):
   BKSPC$=CTRL.H$+UNDRLN$+CTRL.H$:
   CTRL.X$=CHR$(24):ESC$=CHR$(27)
30 PRINT:PRINT"1-Name":
   PRINT"2-Address":PRINT"3-Quit   ";
40 W$=INPUT$(1):
   IF W$<"1"OR W$>"3"
      THEN
         40
      ELSE
         PRINT:ON VAL(W$) GOTO 50,60,70
50 PRINT"Name : ";:INLEN%=20:DEFLT$="N.N.":
   GOSUB 1000:NAM$=BUFF$:GOTO 30
60 PRINT"address : ";:INLEN%=25:DEFLT$="Unknown":
   GOSUB 1000:ADDRESS$=BUFF$:GOTO 30
```

```
70 PRINT:PRINT NAM$,ADDRESS$:
   END

1000 BUFF$="":ERASE.BUFF$=""
1010 PRINT STRING$(INLEN%,UNDRLN$);
          STRING$(INLEN%,CTRL.H$);
1020 W$=INPUT$(1):
     IF W$>=" "AND W$<=CHR$(127)
        THEN
           1100
1030 IF W$=CTRL.H$
        THEN
           IF BUFF$=""
              THEN
                 1020
              ELSE
                 BUFF$=LEFT$(BUFF$,LEN(BUFF$)-1):
                 PRINT BKSPC$;:GOTO 1020
1040 IF W$<>CR.RET$
        THEN
           1060
        ELSE
1050       PRINT STRING$(INLEN%-LEN(BUFF$)," ");:
           IF BUFF$=""
              THEN
                 BUFF$=DEFLT$:
                 FOR I=1 TO INLEN%:
                    PRINT CTRL.H$;:
                 NEXT:PRINT DEFLT$;:RETURN
              ELSE
                 RETURN
1060 IF W$=CTRL.X$
        THEN
           ERASE.BUFF$=BUFF$:
           FOR I=1 TO LEN(BUFF$):
              PRINT BKSPC$;:
           NEXT:BUFF$="":GOTO 1020
1070 IF W$=CTRL.R$
        THEN
           FOR I=1 TO LEN(BUFF$):
              PRINT BKSPC$;:
           NEXT:
           BUFF$=ERASE.BUFF$:PRINT BUFF$;:GOTO 1020
1080 IF W$=ESC$
        THEN
           POP:PRINT STRING$(LEN(BUFF$),CTRL.H$);
           STRING$(INLEN%," "):BUFF$="":GOTO 30
1090 GOTO 1020
1100 IF LEN(BUFF$)=INLEN%
        THEN
           1020
        ELSE
           PRINT W$;:BUFF$=BUFF$+W$:GOTO 1020
```

Program 1.9

1.10 SELECTIVE INPUT

In the previous section, we considered the use of ⟨esc⟩ to return to a menu. As the size of a program grows, so does the number of options and therefore the number of menus. When there is more than one menu, a decision must be made regarding the way to handle the return from input via ⟨esc⟩.

One possible scheme is to assign codes to the different menus and use them as guides to the return locations. As an example, consider a program with two menus, the first of which is assigned the code 1, the second the code 2. The code 0 means no menu, that is, return to command level. (Terminate the program.) When the input subroutine detects the ⟨esc⟩, it executes a POP and looks at the guide number. If the number is one, the program knows it must return to the first menu, of which it has the address; if the number is two, the program must jump to the second menu; and finally, if the number is zero, the program must jump to its final part. (Some actions might need to be done before the actual execution of END.)

Program SELECT has two levels of input. The main menu has two options, which in turn call two menus, each with three options. All of these allows the return to the previous menu. There are, therefore, four different cases: case zero (command level, end of program), case one (main menu), case two (first option), and case three (second option). When the program is at a menu asking which option is selected, it makes sense to input only one character (with INPUT$(1) or INKEY$), unless some of the options need more than one character to indicate the choice. If the option of returning to the previous menu with ⟨esc⟩ is used, it makes sense to have it not only for input of strings or numbers, but for any input, and this is certainly input. Therefore, when analyzing the character entered at the menu level, ⟨esc⟩ must be considered and treated in the same manner as it is in the input subroutine.

At the start of a program, the menu guide should be set to zero, since an ⟨esc⟩ at the first menu means 'jump to command level', i.e., case zero. When one of the two menus is chosen, the guide should be set to level one, since ⟨esc⟩ must return to the first menu. Lastly, when one of the options of the second menus is selected, the guide should be set to the code of the corresponding menu, so that an ⟨esc⟩ during the input subroutine makes the program jump to the corresponding menu. As soon as the input is finished, the guide must be adjusted to the first level, since the program jumps back to the second level of menus.

The actual jump is accomplished by an

ON GUIDE GOTO address 1, address 2, address 3.

```
10 '
                      ** SELECT **
                    Selective menu

20 CTRL.H$=CHR$(8):CR.RET$=CHR$(13):
   UNDRLN$=CHR$(95):CTRL.R$=CHR$(18):
   BKSPC$=CTRL.H$+UNDRLN$+CTRL.H$:
   CTRL.X$=CHR$(24):ESC$=CHR$(27)
30 MENU.RETURN=1:PRINT:PRINT:PRINT"1-Records":
   PRINT"2-Books":PRINT"3-Quit   ";
40 W$=INPUT$(1):
   IF W$=ESC$
     THEN
        130
     ELSE
        IF W$<"1"OR W$>"3"
          THEN
             40
          ELSE
            PRINT:ON VAL(W$) GOTO 50,90,130
50 MENU.RETURN=2:PRINT:PRINT"1-Long Play":
   PRINT"2-Single":PRINT"3-Menu   ";
60 W$=INPUT$(1):
   IF W$=ESC$
     THEN
        30
     ELSE
        IF W$<"1"OR W$>"3"
          THEN
             60
          ELSE
            ON VAL(W$) GOTO 70,80,30
70 PRINT:PRINT"Long play name : ";:INLEN%=20:
   GOSUB 1000:L.P$=BUFF$:GOTO 50
80 PRINT:PRINT"Single's name : ";:INLEN%=20:
   GOSUB 1000:SINGLE$=BUFF$:GOTO 50
90 MENU.RETURN=3:PRINT:PRINT"1-Magazine":
   PRINT"2-Book":PRINT"3-Menu   ";
100 W$=INPUT$(1):
    IF W$=ESC$
      THEN
         30
      ELSE
         IF W$<"1"OR W$>"3"
           THEN
              100
           ELSE
             ON VAL(W$) GOTO 110,120,30
```

```
110 PRINT:PRINT"Magazine's name : ";:INLEN%=15:
    GOSUB 1000:MAGAZINE$=BUFF$:GOTO 90
120 PRINT:PRINT"Book's name : ";:INLEN%=15:
    GOSUB 1000:BOOK$=BUFF$:GOTO 90
130 PRINT:PRINT"Long play : ";L.P$:
    PRINT"Single      : ";SINGLE$:
    PRINT"Magazine    : ";MAGAZINE$:
    PRINT"book        : ";BOOK$:END
1000 BUFF$="":ERASE.BUFF$=""
1010 PRINT STRING$(INLEN%,UNDRLN$);
            STRING$(INLEN%,CTRL.H$);
1020 W$=INPUT$(1):
     IF W$>=" "AND W$<=CHR$(127)
        THEN
           1090
1030 IF W$=CTRL.H$
        THEN
           IF BUFF$=""
              THEN
                 1020
              ELSE
                 BUFF$=LEFT$(BUFF$,LEN(BUFF$)-1):
                 PRINT BKSPC$;:GOTO 1020
1040 IF W$=CR.RET$
        THEN
           PRINT STRING$(INLEN%-LEN(BUFF$)," ");:
           RETURN
1050 IF W$=CTRL.X$
        THEN
           ERASE.BUFF$=BUFF$:
           FOR I=1 TO LEN(BUFF$):
              PRINT BKSPC$;:
           NEXT:BUFF$="":GOTO 1020
1060 IF W$=CTRL.R$
        THEN
           FOR I=1 TO LEN(BUFF$):
              PRINT BKSPC$;:
           NEXT:
           BUFF$=ERASE.BUFF$:PRINT BUFF$;:GOTO 1020
1070 IF W$=ESC$
        THEN
           POP:PRINT STRING$(LEN(BUFF$),CTRL.H$);
           STRING$(INLEN%," "):BUFF$="":
           ON MENU.RETURN GOTO 130,50,90
1080 GOTO 1020
1090 IF LEN(BUFF$)=INLEN%
        THEN
           1020
        ELSE
           PRINT W$;:BUFF$=BUFF$+W$:GOTO 1020
```

Program 1.10

1.11 INPUT WITHOUT
STOPPING THE PROGRAM

All the programs we have so far considered have had to wait until the input was terminated (which was signaled with a ⟨return⟩ or when the specified length was reached) to continue with the next instruction. It does not matter if it takes you one second or one day to answer, because the program will wait patiently and will not do anything until you inform it that you have finished. This also applies to the BASIC commands, INPUT, LINE INPUT, and INPUT$(val).

The function INKEY$ lets you read the keyboard without stopping the program. To see how it works, study Program Fragment 1.1.

```
10 I=1
30 W$=INKEY$:
   IF W$=""
      THEN
         I=I+1:PRINT I;:GOTO 30
Rest of program here.
```

Program Fragment 1.1

As long as W$ is empty, line 30 reads the keyboard over and over again, and I is incremented and printed. If a key is pressed, the corresponding character is assigned to W$, and the program continues. The result is that the program prints a sequence of numbers until a key is pressed, and then continues.

If a key is pressed and the program is busy, the character at the keyboard remains available to the program until the next INKEY$ is executed or until a different key is pressed, in which case the previous one is lost and the new character is the one returned by INKEY$.

If INKEY$ instead of INPUT$(1) is used to fetch characters from the keyboard, the input subroutine can still perform other tasks while it waits for you to press the next key.

In program NONSTOP the W$ = INPUT$(1) of line 1010 of the usual input subroutine has been changed to GOSUB 2000, where an INKEY$ checks the keyboard. If no key has been pressed, the counter C is incremented. When it reaches a value of 101, it is set to 70, and two bell characters are printed. When a key is pressed, line 2000 sets C to 0 and RETURNs from the subroutine with the character typed in W$. That way, every time a key is pressed, validly or invalidly, it resets the counter to zero, and the input subroutine behaves normally. When you let a long time pass between keypresses, the program reminds you with a couple of beeps that it is still waiting.

```
10
                        ** NONSTOP **
                        Non-stop input

20 CTRL.H$=CHR$(8):CR.RET$=CHR$(13):
   UNDRLN$=CHR$(95):CTRL.R$=CHR$(18):
   BKSPC$=CTRL.H$+UNDRLN$+CTRL.H$:
   CTRL.X$=CHR$(24):ESC$=CHR$(27):BELL$=CHR$(7)
30 PRINT"Type your name : ";:INLEN%=20:
   GOSUB 1000:PRINT:PRINT BUFF$:
   END

1000 BUFF$="":PRINT STRING$(INLEN%,UNDRLN$);
                    STRING$(INLEN%,CTRL.H$);
1010 GOSUB 2000:
     IF W$>=" "AND W$<=CHR$(127)
        THEN
           1070
1020 IF W$=CTRL.H$
        THEN
           IF BUFF$=""
              THEN
                 1010
              ELSE
                 BUFF$=LEFT$(BUFF$,LEN(BUFF$)-1):
                 PRINT BKSPC$;:GOTO 1010
1030 IF W$=CR.RET$
        THEN
           PRINT STRING$(INLEN%-LEN(BUFF$)," ");:
           RETURN
1040 IF W$=CTRL.X$
        THEN
           ERASE.BUFF$=BUFF$:
           FOR I=1 TO LEN(BUFF$):
             PRINT BKSPC$;:
           NEXT:GOTO 1000
1050 IF W$=CTRL.R$
        THEN
           FOR I=1 TO LEN(BUFF$):
             PRINT BKSPC$;:
           NEXT:
           BUFF$=ERASE.BUFF$:PRINT BUFF$;:GOTO 1010
1060 GOTO 1010
1070 IF LEN(BUFF$)=INLEN%
        THEN
           1010
        ELSE
           PRINT W$;:BUFF$=BUFF$+W$:GOTO 1010
```

```
2000 W$-INKEY$:
     IF W$<>""
        THEN C=0:RETURN
        ELSE
          C=C+1:
          IF C>100
             THEN
                C=70:PRINT STRING$(2,BELL$);:
                GOTO 2000
             ELSE RETURN
```

Program 1.11

On some terminals the cursor will only be present during the execution of some of the INPUT commands. Thus it will be invisible in program nonstop. If its presence is considered essential, here are two ways to produce it:

1. Choose a character different from the one used in the input line (e.g., an underline when the prompt line is made of spaces, and a hyphen when the prompt line is made of underlines), and print it at the cursor position. In order to have the accepted characters echoed in the right place, it is necessary to type a Ctrl-H before printing the character. This cursor must be erased every time a character is deleted from the field with Ctrl-H or Ctrl-X.

2. If the terminal supports more than the normal supply of attributes (inverse, flashing, increased intensity, etc.), printing a space with a different attribute produces a block that is equivalent to a cursor. A space in flash (or blink mode) is very noticeable. If you want a flashing cursor, and your terminal does not support flash mode, a distinct character (e.g., the underscore or an inverse space) can be printed and deleted at intervals, using a counter to keep track of the time between blinks.

In Sections 1.9 and 1.10, ⟨esc⟩ was used to return to the different menus from the input field. Using the same technique plus INKEY$, it can be guaranteed that the program will return to the previous menu from anywhere if you check the keyboard looking for an ⟨esc⟩ in loops of any kind and in long sequences of instructions. When a long process is interrupted by an ⟨esc⟩ before completion, it is a good idea to return to the menu. To the usual options, a new one should be added allowing the continuation of the process that might have been interrupted by mistake.

If your version of BASIC does not have the function **INKEY$**, you can use INP instead. INP with the keyboard input port number as argument returns the number that corresponds to the ASCII code of the last character typed, but it is not cleared after you read it. If the last character you typed was ⟨return⟩, for example, INP will return 13 until a different key is pressed. To imitate INKEY$, you can decide that a new key has been pressed if the value in INP has changed since the last time you read it. When you must read the same character more than once, type a character with no side effect (a control character not used in the input subroutine).

1.12 INPUT WHILE PROGRAM IS BUSY

There are many situations in which the computer must be kept occupied for a while, and no input can be done. Examples of this are reading a long file, printing a long document, or executing a long loop.

By now, we know how to do input without stopping the program, and it is sometimes useful to have a way to enter data while processing is not yet finished. An easy way to accomplish this is to read the keyboard (via INKEY$) upon every iteration of the repetitive process (every pass through the loop). If there is one character waiting, it can be stored in a string where the previous characters have been kept for later use. If there is no character at the keyboard, only one comparison has been added to the process, and the time performance of the loop will be affected very little. Once the process keeping the computer busy is finished, the rest of the program can continue. In program BUSYINPT, when the input subroutine starts executing, it calls subroutine 2000 to get one character. The string that stores the characters read is called KBD.BUFF$. If it is empty, line 2010 checks the keyboard before RETURNing. Otherwise, the first character in KBD.BUFF$ is copied into W$ and deleted from KBD.BUFF$ with a

KBD.BUFF$ = RIGHT$(KBD.BUFF$,LEN(KBD.BUFF$) − 1)

so that the input subroutine processes the characters in the order of their entry. Before RETURNing from the subroutine, the program reads the keyboard once more, because now it is the input subroutine that is keeping the computer busy. This way, what returns from the subroutine is either an empty W$ when there are no characters ready or the next character that was read, either while the computer was busy or when the input subroutine had not yet finished processing the characters accumulated in the keyboard buffer. When KBD.BUFF$ is empty, the input subroutine behaves normally.

When the process is long, the length of KBD.BUFF$ can reach 255, and an attempt to add one more character will make the program fail by a 'string too long' error. To avoid this, the length can be checked before adding the new character to KDB.BUFF$, but this slows down the process. An alternative way is to let an ON ERROR routine handle the unlikely case of the buffer overflow. When the 'string too long' error code is detected, a message to the effect that any further characters will be ignored is printed, and processing continues.

Program BUSYINPT reads data from a file called "DUMMY" to keep the computer busy and demonstrate the buffering of the keyboard.

```
10 '
                        ** BUSYINPT **
                       Input while busy

15 OPEN"R",1,"DUMMY":FIELD#1,20 AS A$:
      LSET A$="YES INDEED.":PUT 1,1:PUT 1,20
20 CTRL.H$=CHR$(8):CR.RET$=CHR$(13):
      UNDRLN$=CHR$(95):CTRL.R$=CHR$(18):
      BKSPC$=CTRL.H$+UNDRLN$+CTRL.H$:
      CTRL.X$=CHR$(24):RECORD=1
30 PRINT"Type your name : ";:
      FOR I=1 TO 180:
        GOSUB 2000:RECORD=RECORD+1:
        IF RECORD=39
          THEN
            RECORD=1
35    GET 1,RECORD:
      NEXT
40 INLEN%=20:GOSUB 1000:PRINT:PRINT BUFF$:CLOSE:
      END

1000 BUFF$="":PRINT STRING$(INLEN%,95);
                    STRING$(INLEN%,CTRL.H$);
1010 GOSUB 2020:
      IF W$>=" "AND W$<=CHR$(127)
        THEN
          1070
1020 IF W$=CTRL.H$
        THEN
          IF BUFF$=""
            THEN
              1010
            ELSE
              BUFF$=LEFT$(BUFF$,LEN(BUFF$)-1):
              PRINT BKSPC$;:GOTO 1010
1030 IF W$=CR.RET$
        THEN
            PRINT STRING$(INLEN%-LEN(BUFF$)," ");:
            RETURN
1040 IF W$=CTRL.X$
```

```
           THEN
              ERASE.BUFF$=BUFF$:
              FOR I=1 TO LEN(BUFF$):
                 PRINT BKSPC$;:
              NEXT:GOTO 1000
   1050 IF W$=CTRL.R$
           THEN
              FOR I=1 TO LEN(BUFF$):
                 PRINT BKSPC$;:
              NEXT:
              BUFF$=ERASE.BUFF$:PRINT BUFF$;:GOTO 1010
   1060 GOTO 1010
   1070 IF LEN(BUFF$)=INLEN%
           THEN
              1010
           ELSE
              PRINT W$;:BUFF$=BUFF$+W$:GOTO 1010
   2000 X$=INKEY$:
        IF X$<>""
           THEN
              KBD.BUFF$=KBD.BUFF$+X$
   2010 RETURN
   2020 GOSUB 2000:W$="":
        IF KBD.BUFF$=""
           THEN
              RETURN
           ELSE
              W$=LEFT$(KBD.BUFF$,1):
              KBD.BUFF$=
              RIGHT$(KBD.BUFF$,LEN(KBD.BUFF$)-1):
              RETURN
```

Program 1.12

1.13 INPUT WHILE PRINTING

When the computer is used to print long disk files, most of the time is usually taken by the printer, because it cannot keep up with the speed at which the computer produces output. If you need the computer for a process other than printing, you must either wait until it is finished or abort the printing.

If the program that you want to run has a considerable amount of input, a process similar to the one described in program NONSTOP can be used.

Program INPPRINT (for input print) asks for the name of the file to print. The file is OPENed, and the program continues until it reaches the first input. INKEY$ is used to fetch characters from the keyboard, using a counter to keep track of the time elapsed since the last key was pressed. If the counter reaches a certain number, the computer can be considered idle, and the next line of the file can be read and printed.

Notice that if the program ends before the entire file has been printed, the printing must continue, or else part of the file will not be printed. That is why in line 140 the program continues until it detects the EOF.

```
10  '
                         ** INPPRINT **
                      Input while printing

20  CTRL.H$=CHR$(8):CR.RET$=CHR$(13):
    UNDRLN$=CHR$(95):CTRL.R$=CHR$(18):
    BKSPC$=CTRL.H$+UNDRLN$+CTRL.H$:
    CTRL.X$=CHR$(24):ESC$=CHR$(27)
22  BKSPC$=CHR$(8)+"_"+CHR$(8):TRUE=-1:FALSE=0:
    INPUT"FILE TO PRINT ";FILE$:
    INPUT"PRINTER LINE LENGTH ";PRT.LEN:
    WIDTH LPRINT(PRT.LEN):OPEN"I",1,FILE$
30  MENU.RETURN=1:PRINT:PRINT:PRINT"1-Records":
    PRINT"2-Books":PRINT"3-Quit   ";
40  GOSUB 2000:
    IF W$=ESC$
      THEN
        130
      ELSE
        IF W$<"1"OR W$>"3"
          THEN
            40
          ELSE
            PRINT:ON VAL(W$) GOTO 50,90,130
50  MENU.RETURN=2:PRINT:PRINT"1-Long Play":
    PRINT"2-Single":PRINT"3-Menu   ";
60  GOSUB 2000:
    IF W$=ESC$
      THEN
        30
      ELSE
        IF W$<"1"OR W$>"3"
          THEN
            60
          ELSE
            ON VAL(W$) GOTO 70,80,30
70  PRINT:PRINT"Long play name : ";:INLEN%=20:
    GOSUB 1000:L.P$=BUFF$:GOTO 50
80  PRINT:PRINT"Single's name : ";:INLEN%=20:
    GOSUB 1000:SINGLE$=BUFF$:GOTO 50
90  MENU.RETURN=3:PRINT:PRINT"1-Magazine":
    PRINT"2-Book":PRINT"3-Menu   ";
100 GOSUB 2000:
    IF W$=ESC$
```

```
          THEN
            30
          ELSE
            IF  W$<"1"OR W$>"3"
               THEN
                 100
               ELSE
                 ON VAL(W$) GOTO 110,120,30
110 PRINT:PRINT"Magazine's name : ";:INLEN%=15:
     GOSUB 1000:MAGAZINE$=BUFF$:GOTO 90
120 PRINT:PRINT"Book's name : ";:INLEN%=15:
    GOSUB 1000:BOOK$=BUFF$:GOTO 90
130 PRINT:PRINT"Long play : ";L.P$:
      PRINT"Single     : ";SINGLE$:
      PRINT"Magazine   : ";MAGAZINE$:
      PRINT"book       : ";BOOK$
140 WHILE NOT DONE.PRT:
       GOSUB 2000:
     WEND:END

1000 BUFF$="":ERASE.BUFF$=""
1010 PRINT STRING$(INLEN%,UNDRLN$);
              STRING$(INLEN%,CTRL.H$);
1020 GOSUB 2000:
      IF  W$>=" "AND W$<=CHR$(127)
         THEN
           1090
1030 IF  W$=CTRL.H$
        THEN
           IF  BUFF$=""
              THEN
                1020
              ELSE
                BUFF$=LEFT$(BUFF$,LEN(BUFF$)-1):
                PRINT BKSPC$;:GOTO 1020
1040 IF  W$=CR.RET$
        THEN
          PRINT STRING$(INLEN%-LEN(BUFF$)," ");:
          RETURN
1050 IF  W$=CTRL.X$
        THEN
          ERASE.BUFF$=BUFF$:
          FOR I=1 TO LEN(BUFF$):
             PRINT BKSPC$;:
          NEXT:BUFF$="":GOTO 1020
1060 IF  W$=CTRL.R$
        THEN
          FOR I=1 TO LEN(BUFF$):
             PRINT BKSPC$;:
          NEXT:
          BUFF$=ERASE.BUFF$:PRINT BUFF$;:GOTO 1020
1070 IF  W$=ESC$
```

```
          THEN
             POP:PRINT STRING$(LEN(BUFF$),CTRL.H$);
                       STRING$(INLEN%," "):BUFF$="":
             ON MENU.RETURN GOTO 130,50,90
1080 GOTO 1020
1090 IF LEN(BUFF$)=INLEN%
          THEN
             1020
          ELSE
             PRINT W$;:BUFF$=BUFF$+W$:GOTO 1020
2000 W$=INKEY$:
        IF W$<>""
          THEN C=0:RETURN
          ELSE
             C=C+1:
             IF C>25 AND NOT DONE.PRT
                THEN C=20:GOSUB 3000:GOTO 2000
                ELSE RETURN
3000 IF PTR.BUFF$<>""
          THEN 3010
          ELSE
             IF EOF(1)
                THEN
                   DONE.PRT=TRUE:CLOSE 1:RETURN
                ELSE
                   LINE INPUT#1,PTR.BUFF$
3010 IF LEN(PTR.BUFF$)>PRT.LEN
          THEN
             TEMP$=LEFT$(PTR.BUFF$,PRT.LEN):
             PTR.BUFF$=
             RIGHT$(PTR.BUFF$,LEN(PTR.BUFF$)-PRT.LEN):
             LPRINT TEMP$
          ELSE
             LPRINT PTR.BUFF$:PTR.BUFF$=""
3020 RETURN
```

Program 1.13

1.14 SIGNED NUMBERS WITH DECIMAL POINT

In this section we are going to study a numeric input subroutine that will accept a sign and a decimal point.

Several points must be considered here. First, when the number has a decimal point, a second one must be considered invalid and therefore must be rejected. Second, the plus and minus signs must be mutually exclusive, since a number normally cannot have two signs. Therefore, a second sign must not be accepted. Third, a decision must be made regarding the number of decimal digits. In program FLPTNUM (for floating-point number), only two will be accepted, as when working with dollars and cents.

The input subroutine of program FLPTNUM initializes DEC.CNT (the counter of the number of decimal digits entered so far) to zero, SIGN (the Boolean variable that indicates whether a sign has been entered) to FALSE, and POINT (the variable that indicates whether a decimal point has been entered) to FALSE. When Ctrl-H is typed, the following cases must be considered:

1. If BUFF$ is empty, nothing must be done.

2. If the last character in BUFF$ is a point, POINT must be set to FALSE, because the point is deleted, and DEC.CNT must be set to zero, since there are no decimal digits after this deletion.

3. If the last character in BUFF$ is not a point, but POINT is TRUE, which means that the character to delete is a decimal digit, DEC.CNT must be decremented by one.

Since the sign will always be the first character in BUFF$, it does not pose a problem with Ctrl-H.

Line 1070 deals with the point. If POINT is TRUE, BUFF$ already has one point and this new one must be ignored. Otherwise, this is the first one, and POINT must be set to TRUE if BUFF$ has fewer characters than specified in INLEN%.

When line 1080 detects a sign, it checks whether BUFF$ is empty. If it is, it accepts the sign; otherwise, it rejects it.

Before a number is added to BUFF$, not only the number of characters, but also the number of decimal digits, in BUFF$ must be checked. If DEC.CNT is equal to 3, no more digits can be accepted.

```
10 '
                        ** FLPTNUM **
            Floating point numbers with '.' and '-,+'

20 CTRL.H$=CHR$(8):CR.RET$=CHR$(13):
   UNDRLN$=CHR$(95):CTRL.R$=CHR$(18):
   BKSPC$=CTRL.H$+UNDRLN$+CTRL.H$:CTRL.X$=CHR$(24)
22 BKSPC$=CHR$(8)+"_"+CHR$(8):TRUE=-1:FALSE=0
30 PRINT:PRINT"Cost per unit $ ";:INLEN%=9:
   GOSUB 1000:PRINT:PRINT BUFF$:
   END

1000 DEC.CNT=0:BUFF$="":SIGN=FALSE:POINT=FALSE:
     PRINT STRING$(INLEN%,UNDRLN$);
           STRING$(INLEN%,CTRL.H$);
1010 W$=INPUT$(1):
     IF W$>="0"AND W$<="9"
```

```
          THEN
             1100
1020 IF W$<>CTRL.H$
          THEN
             1040
          ELSE
1030         IF BUFF$=""
                THEN
                   1010
                ELSE
                   W$=RIGHT$(BUFF$,1):
                   BUFF$=LEFT$(BUFF$,LEN(BUFF$)-1):
                   PRINT BKSPC$;:
                   IF W$="."
                      THEN POINT=FALSE:DEC.CNT=0
1035               IF POINT
                      THEN
                         DEC.CNT=DEC.CNT-1:GOTO 1010
                      ELSE
                         1010
1040 IF W$=CR.RET$
          THEN
             PRINT STRING$(INLEN%-LEN(BUFF$)," ");:
             RETURN
1050 IF W$=CTRL.X$
          THEN
             ERASE.BUFF$=BUFF$:
             FOR I=1 TO LEN(BUFF$):
                PRINT BKSPC$;:
             NEXT:GOTO 1000
1060 IF W$=CTRL.R$
          THEN
             FOR I=1 TO LEN(BUFF$):
                PRINT BKSPC$;:
             NEXT:
             BUFF$=ERASE.BUFF$:PRINT BUFF$;:GOTO 1010
1070 IF W$="."
          THEN
             IF POINT
                THEN
                   1010
                ELSE
                   IF LEN(BUFF$)=INLEN%
                      THEN
                         1010
                      ELSE
                         POINT=TRUE:GOTO 1100
1080 IF W$="-"OR W$="+"
          THEN
             IF BUFF$>""
                THEN
                   1010
                ELSE
                   1100
```

```
1090 GOTO 1010
1100 IF LEN(BUFF$)=INLEN% OR DEC.CNT=3
        THEN
            1010
        ELSE
          PRINT W$;:BUFF$=BUFF$+W$:
          IF POINT
            THEN
                DEC.CNT=DEC.CNT+1:GOTO 1010
            ELSE
                1010
```

Program 1.14

1.15 SOFTWARE REPEAT

Most modern terminals have a way to repeat a key, either by keeping it depressed, or with the help of a special repeat key. Some do not have that feature, and in some others the repetition is slow or the key must be pressed for a long time before it starts repeating. (Here, long can be as little as two seconds, but with the current speed of computers, most people do not want to wait even that long).

The key repetition feature is particularly useful to fill in long chains of input rapidly when a program is being debugged. In this section, we will show the way to make the input subroutine repeat a key with the help of INKEY$.

In program SOFTREPT, when a character is needed by the input subroutine, line 2000 (called by line 1010) checks the keyboard with INKEY$. If the key pressed is a Ctrl-A, the Boolean variable WAIT.CHAR is set to TRUE, so that the next character typed is copied in the variable REPEAT$. When the key pressed is not a Ctrl-A, and WAIT.CHAR is FALSE, the subroutine returns with the character received in W$ so that the input subroutine can process it.

If INKEY$ returns and empty string (which will be the case most of the time), line 3000 checks the variable REPEAT$. If it is not empty, its contents are copied into W$, and the subroutine RETURNs just as if the character in REPEAT$ had been typed at the keyboard. If REPEAT$ is empty, the keyboard is read again.

```
10 '
                    ** SOFTREPT **
                   Software repeat

20 CTRL.H$=CHR$(8):CR.RET$=CHR$(13):
   UNDRLN$=CHR$(95):CTRL.R$=CHR$(18):
   BKSPC$=CTRL.H$+UNDRLN$+CTRL.H$:TRUE=-1:
   CTRL.X$=CHR$(24):CTRL.A$=CHR$(1):FALSE=0
```

```
 21 HOME
 30 FOR J=1 TO 10:
      PRINT"Name : ";:INLEN%=25:
      GOSUB 1000:PRINT"    Address : ";:INLEN%=30:
      GOSUB 1000:PRINT:PRINT"Telephone : ";:
      INLEN%=7:GOSUB 1000:PRINT:
    NEXT:
    END

1000 ERASE.BUFF$=""
1005 BUFF$="":PRINT STRING$(INLEN%,UNDRLN$);:
      FOR I=1 TO INLEN%:
        PRINT CTRL.H$;:
      NEXT
1010 GOSUB 2000:
      IF W$>=" "AND W$<=CHR$(127)
        THEN
          1070
1020 IF W$=CTRL.H$
        THEN
          IF BUFF$=""
            THEN
              1010
            ELSE
              BUFF$=LEFT$(BUFF$,LEN(BUFF$)-1):
              PRINT BKSPC$;:GOTO 1010
1030 IF W$=CR.RET$
        THEN
          PRINT STRING$(INLEN%-LEN(BUFF$)," ");:
          RETURN
1040 IF W$=CTRL.X$
        THEN
          ERASE.BUFF$=BUFF$:
          FOR I=1 TO LEN(BUFF$):
            PRINT BKSPC$;:
          NEXT:GOTO 1005
1050 IF W$=CTRL.R$
        THEN
          FOR I=1 TO LEN(BUFF$):
            PRINT BKSPC$;:
          NEXT:
          BUFF$=ERASE.BUFF$:PRINT BUFF$;:GOTO 1010
1060 GOTO 1010
1070 BUFF$=BUFF$+W$:
      IF LEN(BUFF$)=INLEN%
        THEN
          PRINT W$;STRING$(INLEN%-LEN(BUFF$)," ");:
          RETURN
        ELSE
          PRINT W$;:GOTO 1010
2000 W$=INKEY$:
      IF W$=""
        THEN
          IF REPEAT$<>""
```

```
                THEN
                   W$=REPEAT$:RETURN
                ELSE
                   2000
           ELSE
  2010        IF  W$=CTRL.A$
                THEN
                   WAIT.CHAR=TRUE:GOTO  2000
                ELSE
                   IF  WAIT.CHAR
                     THEN
                       WAIT.CHAR=FALSE:REPEAT$=W$:
                       GOTO  2000
                     ELSE
                       REPEAT$="":RETURN
```

Program 1.15

Notice that if Ctrl-A is pressed while the repeat is active, the next character typed will be repeated, but the current repeat will not be interrupted.

1.16 UPPER/LOWER CASE CONTROL

Since it is the program that is echoing to the screen, and not the language itself, we can process every character before printing and adding it to BUFF$.

To handle characters, the computer assigns a number to each letter, number, and symbol, according to a code[2] called ASCII (American Standard Code for Information Interchange; the table of equivalences between ASCII codes and characters can be found in Appendix A). The code for ⟨return⟩, for example, is 13. The function CHR$( ) returns the character that corresponds to the number between the parentheses, and the function ASC( ) returns the code of the string provided. The code for uppercase "A" is 65, and that for lowercase "a" is 97. The difference between these two numbers is 32, and this "distance" is kept constant throughout the alphabet. (ASC("p") − ASC("P") = 32.) This means that if you take an uppercase character and add 32 to the ASCII code that you get with the ASC function, the character that corresponds to the resulting number is the lowercase character of the original letter. Here is an example:

---

[2]There are other codes, such as the EBCDIC, but the ASCII is becoming more and more the standard in small- and medium-sized computers.

$$ASC(\text{``A''}) = 65$$
$$65 + 32 = 97$$
$$CHR\$(97) = \text{``a''}$$

In program UPLOCASE (for upper and lower case), the following characters have been chosen to control the different case modes:

Ctrl-Q Switches the input between normal mode, upper case only, and lower case only.

Ctrl-E Makes every letter in the input field reverse mode; that is, every uppercase letter will become lower case, and vice versa.

The variable CASE will keep track of the current mode: (1) normal, (2) uppercase, and (3) lowercase. When line 1070 detects a Ctrl-Q, it switches to the next case in the sequence 1, 2, 3, 1, 2, etc. Line 1110 checks the length of BUFF$. If there is room for the new valid character, it uses CASE to jump to three different locations. Line 1140 treats the normal case, in which the character is echoed and added to BUFF$ as entered. Line 1120 treats the uppercase: if the character is in the range "a" . . "z", it is converted to an uppercase letter (by subtracting 32 from its ASCII code), echoed, and added to BUFF$. Notice that if the character is not a lowercase letter, nothing is done to it. Finally, line 1130 converts uppercase letters to lowercase.

When Ctrl-E is detected by line 1080, a loop analyzes every character in BUFF$. Uppercase letters are converted to lowercase, and lowercase to uppercase; the numbers and symbols are not touched. When the entire string has been processed, the current input field is erased by printing as many BCKSPC$'s as there are characters in BUFF$, and the new BUFF$ is printed.

```
10 '
                     ** UPLOCASE **
                   Upper/lower case

        Ctrl.Q  :  Case 1 :  Upper/lower case as typed
                   Case 2 :  All upper case
                   Case 3 :  All lower case

        Ctrl.E  :  Reverse case

 20 CTRL.H$=CHR$(8):CR.RET$=CHR$(13):
    UNDRLN$=CHR$(95):CTRL.R$=CHR$(18):
    BKSPC$=CTRL.H$+UNDRLN$+CTRL.H$:
    CTRL.X$=CHR$(24):CTRL.Q$=CHR$(17):
    CTRL.E$=CHR$(5)
```

```
 30 PRINT"Type your name : ";:INLEN%=20:
    GOSUB 1000:PRINT:PRINT BUFF$:
    END

1000 CASE=1
1010 BUFF$="":PRINT STRING$(INLEN%,UNDRLN$);
                    STRING$(INLEN%,CTRL.H$);
1020 W$=INPUT$(1):
     IF W$>=" "AND W$<=CHR$(127)
        THEN
           1110
1030 IF W$=CTRL.H$
        THEN
           IF BUFF$=""
              THEN
                 1020
              ELSE
                 BUFF$=LEFT$(BUFF$,LEN(BUFF$)-1):
                 PRINT BKSPC$;:GOTO 1020
1040 IF W$=CR.RET$
        THEN
           PRINT STRING$(INLEN%-LEN(BUFF$)," ");:
           RETURN
1050 IF W$=CTRL.X$
        THEN
           ERASE.BUFF$=BUFF$:
           FOR I=1 TO LEN(BUFF$):
              PRINT BKSPC$;:
           NEXT:GOTO 1010
1060 IF W$=CTRL.R$
        THEN
           FOR I=1 TO LEN(BUFF$):
              PRINT BKSPC$;:
           NEXT:
           BUFF$=ERASE.BUFF$:PRINT BUFF$;:
           GOTO 1020
1070 IF W$=CTRL.Q$
        THEN
           CASE=CASE+1:
           IF CASE=4

              THEN
                 CASE=1
1080 IF W$<>CTRL.E$
        THEN
           1020
        ELSE
           FOR I=1 TO LEN(BUFF$):
              W$=MID$(BUFF$,I,1):
              IF W$>="A"AND W$<="Z"
                 THEN MID$(BUFF$,I,1)=CHR$(ASC(W$)+32)
                 ELSE
1090                IF W$>="a"AND W$<="z"
                       THEN
```

```
                          MID$(BUFF$,I,1)=
                                      CHR$(ASC(W$)-32)
   1100       NEXT:
              PRINT STRING$(LEN(BUFF$),CTRL.H$);BUFF$;:
              GOTO 1020
   1110 IF LEN(BUFF$)=INLEN%
          THEN
              1020
          ELSE
              ON CASE GOTO 1140,1120,1130
   1120 IF W$>="a"AND W$<="z"
          THEN
              W$=CHR$(ASC(W$)-32):GOTO 1140
          ELSE
              1140
   1130 IF W$>="A"AND W$<="Z"
          THEN
              W$=CHR$(ASC(W$)+32)
   1140 PRINT W$;:BUFF$=BUFF$+W$:GOTO 1020
```

Program 1.16

1.17 NUMBERS WITH FORMAT

A more elegant way to do input of numbers than the one shown in program FLPTNUM of Section 1.14 is to show the numbers with a format that facilitates their comprehension. It is much easier to visualize a number if the decimal point and the decimal digits are displayed and if every group of three integer digits is separated from every other such group by a comma, even if some or all these digits are zeros.

To make this input subroutine as close as possible to the way most calculators handle input, a few points have to be considered besides those discussed in Section 1.14. These points deal with the way to keep track of the number, but say nothing of the way to update the display, which will be treated later. Program NUMFORM does the input of single-precision numbers with two decimal digits. The number sent in INLEN% is considered to be the total number of digits, without counting the decimal point, i.e., if INLEN% = 8, up to six integer and two decimal digits will be accepted.

When a digit is accepted and added to BUFF$, one of two counters has to be updated: either the number of integer digits (those to the left of the decimal point) if there is no decimal point, or the number of decimal digits.

When the character accepted is the point, the variable POINT must be set to TRUE to preclude accepting a second point.

When the character is a minus sign, one of two things must be done (the minus sign is used here as the +/− key of calculators, that is, every time it is pressed, the number changes sign): If the first character in BUFF$ is a minus sign, it must be deleted; otherwise, a minus sign must be added to the left of BUFF$.

When a character is to be deleted, one of three variables must be Updated. If the character deleted is the decimal point, the Boolean variable POINT has to be set to FALSE. If there is no decimal point in BUFF$, the counter of the integer digits must be decremented. Otherwise, the counter of the number of decimal digits must be decremented.

When Ctrl-X is used to delete the entire number, not only the contents of BUFF$, but also the counters of integer and decimal digits as well as the indicator as to whether there is or not a point in BUFF$, must be stored in ERASE.BUFF$. If this is not done, when the number is restored with Ctrl-R, the behavior of the program may not correspond with the number displayed.

Since the number will be displayed with a format which is easy to visualize, instead of printing every valid digit as it is typed, the entire number will be printed using PRINT USING every time there is a change. To print the number in the same place every time, the cursor must be returned to the beginning of the field before executing PRINT USING. Unlike the previous programs, the number of Ctrl-H's to print here is constant, since the number printed will always have the same length. The length of BUFF$ has nothing to do with what is displayed, since even an empty BUFF$ will make a 0.00 be printed. The length of the PRINT USING field must be counted by hand and changed every time a different format is used. Program Fragment 1.2 lets you count the number of characters printed with the format specified in line 10.

```
10 FORM$="#######,.##"
20 ?"123456789 123456789"
30 PRINT USING FORM$;0
```

Program Fragment 1.2

The use of program NUMFORM with variables of double precision slows down the input subroutine substantially because PRINT USING with double-precision values is slow. If you find that this delay is too great, use the alternative method discussed in Exercise 1.12.

```
10  '
                  ** NUMFORM **
              Numbers with FORMAT

15 HOME
20 CTRL.H$=CHR$(8):CR.RET$=CHR$(13):
   UNDRLN$=CHR$(95):CTRL.R$=CHR$(18):
```

```
    BKSPC$=CTRL.H$+UNDRLN$+CTRL.H$:
    CTRL.X$=CHR$(24):TRUE=-1:FALSE=0:
    RET.CUR$=STRING$(11,CTRL.H$)
30 PRINT"Cost per unit $ ";:INLEN%=8:
    GOSUB 1000:PRINT:V=VAL(BUFF$):
    PRINT USING"#######,.##";V:GOTO 30:
    END

1000 PREV.INT=0:PREV.PNT=FALSE:PREV.DEC=0:
      ERASE.BUFF$="":BUFF$="":
      PRINT STRING$(11," ");:GOSUB 1110
1005 INT.CNT=0:POINT=FALSE:DEC.CNT=0:BUFF$=""
1010 W$=INPUT$(1):
      IF W$>="0"AND W$<="9"
        THEN
          1100
1020 IF W$<>CTRL.H$
        THEN
          1040
        ELSE
1030     IF BUFF$=""
            THEN
              1010
            ELSE
              W$=RIGHT$(BUFF$,1):
              BUFF$=LEFT$(BUFF$,LEN(BUFF$)-1):
              GOSUB 1110:
              IF W$="."
                THEN
                  POINT=FALSE:DEC.CNT=0:GOTO 1010
1035         IF POINT
                THEN
                  DEC.CNT=DEC.CNT-1:GOTO 1010
                ELSE
                  INT.CNT=INT.CNT-1:GOTO 1010
1040 IF W$=CR.RET$
        THEN
          RETURN
1050 IF W$=CTRL.X$
        THEN
          ERASE.BUFF$=BUFF$:BUFF$="":
          PREV.INT=INT.CNT:
          PREV.PNT=POINT:PREV.DEC=DEC.CNT:
          GOSUB 1110:GOTO 1005
1060 IF W$=CTRL.R$
        THEN
          BUFF$=ERASE.BUFF$:POINT=PREV.PNT:
          INT.CNT=PREV.INT:DEC.CNT=PREV.DEC:
          GOSUB 1110:GOTO 1010
1070 IF W$="."
        THEN
          IF POINT
            THEN 1010
            ELSE
              IF INT.CNT=INLEN%-2
```

```
                            THEN
                               1010
                            ELSE
                               POINT=TRUE:GOTO 1100
       1080 IF W$="-"
               THEN
                   IF LEFT$(BUFF$,1)="-"
                       THEN
                           BUFF$=RIGHT$(BUFF$,LEN(BUFF$)-1):
                           GOSUB 1110:GOTO 1010
                       ELSE
                           BUFF$="-"+BUFF$:GOSUB 1110:
                           GOTO 1010
               ELSE
                   1010
       1100 IF INT.CNT=INLEN%-2 OR DEC.CNT=3
               THEN 1010
               ELSE
                   IF W$="0"AND VAL(BUFF$)=0
                       THEN
                           1010
                       ELSE
       1105                BUFF$=BUFF$+W$:GOSUB 1110:
                           IF POINT
                               THEN
                                   DEC.CNT=DEC.CNT+1:GOTO 1010
                               ELSE
                                   INT.CNT=INT.CNT+1:GOTO 1010
       1110 V=VAL(BUFF$):PRINT RET.CUR$;:
            PRINT USING"#######,.##";V;:RETURN
```

Program 1.17

1.18 BATCH

Most of the sophisticated operating systems permit the redefinition of the source of the input: you can specify that, for a certain program, the input be taken not from the keyboard but from a file, or even from a different piece of hardware (e.g., card reader, paper tape, etc.). This can be particularly useful in programs that must perform many calculations between inputs and therefore run for a long time. A file with all the input is created with an editor, and the computer is left alone to process the input as it needs it.

The bad news is that, unfortunately, those operating systems are usually available only in big computers. The good news is that program INBATCH will do the job for you.

In every previous input subroutine we fetched one character, analyzed it, and took the corresponding action before getting the next one. But the input subroutine did not care where that character came from, as long as it returned in W$.

Line 25 executes an ON ERROR GOTO command and then OPENs the file BATCH.TXT. (You can make your program ask both for the name of the file and whether the input is going to come from the keyboard.) The Boolean variable BATCH is set to TRUE, and the program continues. In line 2000, since BATCH is TRUE, a character is read from the file using INPUT$(1,1), where the first 1 corresponds to the number of characters to read (one in this case), and the second 1 specifies the file. Subroutine 2000 RETURNs with the character in W$. (The jump to line 2030 will be explained later.) EOF(1) tests whether there is at least one character in the file before trying to read it. If the file is finished, execution continues at line 2010, which reads the character from the keyboard. This way, the program can be run partly with the input taken from a file, and if the file has fewer characters than the program requires, the rest are read from the keyboard.

If the file does not exist, the attempt to OPEN it causes a 'file not found' error, which makes the program jump to line 5000, where the file is CLOSEd and BATCH is set to FALSE. From that moment on, subroutine 2000 takes all the input from the keyboard.

When the program is run for the first time, the error routine CLOSEs the file and reOPENs it, this time in the ''O'' mode, to write to it. Line 2030 sends every character that is entered at the keyboard to the file, so that the next time you run the program, it will duplicate the session. Since every character ends up in the file (even control characters), when the program is run using this file as input, the behavior will be exactly the same as when the original program was run.

```
10 '
                        ** INBATCH **
                       Input with Batch

20 CTRL.H$=CHR$(8):CR.RET$=CHR$(13):
   UNDRLN$=CHR$(95):CTRL.R$=CHR$(18):
   BKSPC$=CTRL.H$+UNDRLN$+CTRL.H$:
   CTRL.X$=CHR$(24):TRUE=-1:FALSE=0
21 HOME
25 ON ERROR GOTO 5000:
   OPEN"I",1,"BATCH":
   BATCH=TRUE
30 FOR J=1 TO 10:
       PRINT"Name : ";:INLEN%=25:GOSUB 1000:
       PRINT"   Address : ";:INLEN%=30:GOSUB 1000:
       PRINT:PRINT"Telephone : ";:INLEN%=7:
       GOSUB 1000:PRINT:
   NEXT:
   END
```

```
1000 ERASE.BUFF$=""
1005 BUFF$="":PRINT STRING$(INLEN%,UNDRLN$);:
     FOR I=1 TO INLEN%:
       PRINT CTRL.H$;:
     NEXT
1010 GOSUB 2000:
     IF W$>=" "AND W$<=CHR$(127)
       THEN
         1070
1020 IF W$=CTRL.H$
       THEN
         IF BUFF$=""
           THEN
             1010
           ELSE
             BUFF$=LEFT$(BUFF$,LEN(BUFF$)-1):
             PRINT BKSPC$;:GOTO 1010
1030 IF W$=CR.RET$
       THEN
         PRINT STRING$(INLEN%-LEN(BUFF$)," ");:
         RETURN
1040 IF W$=CTRL.X$
       THEN
         ERASE.BUFF$=BUFF$:
         FOR I=1 TO LEN(BUFF$):
           PRINT BKSPC$;:
         NEXT:GOTO 1005
1050 IF W$=CTRL.R$
       THEN
         FOR I=1 TO LEN(BUFF$):
           PRINT BKSPC$;:
         NEXT:
         BUFF$=ERASE.BUFF$:PRINT BUFF$;:GOTO 1010
1060 GOTO 1010
1070 BUFF$=BUFF$+W$:
     IF LEN(BUFF$)=INLEN%
       THEN
         PRINT W$;STRING$(INLEN%-LEN(BUFF$)," ");:
         RETURN
       ELSE
         PRINT W$;:GOTO 1010
2000 IF BATCH
       THEN
         IF NOT EOF(1)
           THEN
             W$=INPUT$(1,1):GOTO 2030
           ELSE 2010
       ELSE
2010     W$=INPUT$(1):
         IF W$=""
           THEN
             2010
2030 IF BATCH
```

```
        THEN
          RETURN
        ELSE
          PRINT#1,W$;:RETURN
 5000 IF ERR=53 AND ERL=25
        THEN
          CLOSE:OPEN"O",1,"BATCH":BATCH=FALSE:
          RESUME 30
 5010 ON ERROR GOTO 0:RESUME
```

Program 1.18

If you keep a disk copy of the input every time the program is run, you will be able to reconstruct the session and analyze it whenever an error occurs. Sometimes only very specific data make a program fail, and when the computer is operated by a person other than the programmer, it is usually impossible to know exactly what made the program fail. To make sure that the copy of the input that caused the error is not deleted, you can include in the error routine a part that renames the batch file.

1.19 PREDEFINED COMMANDS

In Sections 1.9 and 1.10 we talked about menus. An alternative way to provide instructions from a program is to have a set of commands whose name must be typed to execute the corresponding action. An example of this is the way you type RUN to execute the program in memory. (BASIC is a program that accepts commands in just this manner.)

Just as you can use the question mark to mean PRINT, you can make your input subroutine recognize certain shorthand versions of your commands and provide the corresponding string.

Program DEFCOMM responds to four of these predefined functions in lines 1012 through 1018. It is only a demonstration of the way to produce the effect described, and the commands are not really executed.

When Ctrl-S is typed, the input subroutine prints "SEARCH", adds it to BUFF$, and waits until you press return . The subroutine does not RETURN immediately, in order to let you change the command in case of a mistake. Since both the screen and BUFF$ are updated, there is no way to tell whether the command was entered directly via the keyboard or obtained from the shorthand version.

Ctrl-D answers with "DELETE" and Ctrl-I with "INSERT". Ctrl-L answers with "LOAD", an automatic return , and the new question "FILENAME:", a prompt for the name of the file to load. In this case, when the subroutine RETURNs with the filename, it has to somehow tell the program that what comes is not a command, but the name of a file that must be loaded. This can be done with a Boolean variable. (If you use LOAD as a variable name, you will get a 'syntax error' message, because it is a reserved word. One way to circumvent this situation is to add a dot to LOAD. The same applies to every reserved word.) Since the subroutine practically calls itself (the command LOAD, inside the subroutine, jumps to the beginning of the input subroutine for the file name), a way must be thought of to turn off the LOAD flag.

Notice that when BUFF$ is not empty, none of the commands works, since it does not make sense to have any characters to the left of the commands.

```
10 '
                        ** DEFCOMM **
                        Define commands

20 CTRL.H$=CHR$(8):CR.RET$=CHR$(13):
   BKSPC$=CTRL.H$+" "+CTRL.H$:CTRL.R$=CHR$(18):
   CTRL.X$=CHR$(24):CTRL.Y$=CHR$(25):
   CTRL.S$=CHR$(19):CTRL.D$=CHR$(4):
   CTRL.I$=CHR$(9):CTRL.L$=CHR$(12)
30 PRINT"Command : ";:INLEN%=20:
   GOSUB 1000:PRINT:PRINT BUFF$:
   END

1000 ERASE.BUFF$=""
1005 BUFF$=""
1010 W$=INPUT$(1):
     IF W$>=" "AND W$<=CHR$(127)
        THEN
           1070
1012 IF W$=CTRL.S$ AND BUFF$=""
        THEN
           BUFF$="SEARCH":PRINT BUFF$;:GOTO 1010
1014 IF W$=CTRL.D$ AND BUFF$=""
        THEN
           BUFF$="DELETE":PRINT BUFF$;:GOTO 1010
1016 IF W$=CTRL.I$ AND BUFF$=""
        THEN
           BUFF$="INSERT":PRINT BUFF$;:GOTO 1010
1018 IF W$=CTRL.L$ AND BUFF$=""
        THEN
           PRINT"LOAD":PRINT" FILENAME : ";:
           GOTO 1010
1020 IF W$=CTRL.H$
        THEN
           IF BUFF$=""
```

```
              THEN
                 1010
              ELSE
                 BUFF$=LEFT$(BUFF$,LEN(BUFF$)-1):
                 PRINT BKSPC$;:GOTO 1010
1030 IF W$=CR.RET$
         THEN
             RETURN
1040 IF W$=CTRL.X$
         THEN
             ERASE.BUFF$=BUFF$:
             FOR I=1 TO LEN(BUFF$):
                PRINT BKSPC$;:
             NEXT:GOTO 1005
1050 IF W$=CTRL.R$
         THEN
             FOR I=1 TO LEN(BUFF$):
                PRINT BKSPC$;:
             NEXT:
             BUFF$=ERASE.BUFF$:PRINT BUFF$;:GOTO 1010
1060 GOTO 1010
1070 IF LEN(BUFF$)=INLEN%
         THEN
             1010
         ELSE
             PRINT W$;:BUFF$=BUFF$+W$:GOTO 1010
```

Program 1.19

If you have input fields shorter than some of the commands, you should check whether the command name will fit. It is does not, you should reject the command.

Exercises

1. Rewrite program RSTRLINE (Section 1.6) so that Ctrl-R restores not just one string, but several, in the reverse order in which they were deleted. (The next to be restored will be the most recently deleted that has not yet been restored.) This can be done easily if you use an array of strings instead of a single ERASE.BUFF$ and 'stack' the deletions. A numeric variable can be used as a pointer to store the index of the highest string in the array. This pointer will go up in the array as more deletions are stored, and down as they are restored. Such a structure is called a *stack* and is used, for example, to keep the return addresses of subroutines.

2. Rewrite program BUSYINP (Section 1.12) so that it

    a. echoes the characters, including backspace, delete-line, and restore-line, as they are typed.

    b. does the same as a, except that it jumps to the next input field when ⟨return⟩ is entered.

3. Rewrite program INBATCH, adding a command that will switch between keyboard and file input. When reading a file, a switch to keyboard input should 'flush' one character of the file every time a valid one is entered at the keyboard, or else the return to the file will find fields that will not correspond with what is expected.

4. Add some editing commands to any of the input subroutines. Be sure to include right and left nondestructive cursor movement, as well as insertion and deletion of one character anywhere in the input field. If your terminal does not support right nondestructive cursor movement, you can simply print the character at the cursor position, and it will automatically be moved to the right.

5. Write a program to do the input of several fields, using MENURET (Section 1.9) plus two commands: one to return the cursor to the first field in the screen, and another one to jump back to the previous field. To do this, you need to know the coordinates of every field and have direct cursor addressing.

6. Write an input subroutine that can be switched from numeric to alphanumeric from the program and from the keyboard.

7. Change the program of Exercise 6 so that when a particular key is pressed, part of the keyboard becomes a numeric pad. (The keys for the numbers are in groups of three, as in most calculators). If your terminal does not have such a pad, this will make the input of numbers easier and faster.

8. Write an input subroutine that will delete and restore the field as in program RSTRLINE (Section 1.6). When you jump to a different field, Ctrl-R should not restore the deletions of the previous field. However, a special key will, after checking whether this new field is big enough to accept the said restoration.

9. Computers communicate with peripherals (printers, video terminals, etc.) through special locations called 'ports.' The function INP(⟨port number⟩) returns the contents of the specified port, and OUT(port,value) sends ⟨value⟩ to the specified port. OUT can be used for output to the printer as INKEY$ is used for input from the keyboard: one character can be sent, and the program will continue immediately. Most printers return a 'ready' signal to a port. If you can find the printer ports (output and ready/busy); you should be able to find the corresponding ports in your computer manuals, write a program that will do output while busy, one character at a time. With these commands, you can make printing as transparent to the user as input while busy.

10. If you make a mistake when you are storing input characters while the computer is busy, there is no way to correct it, especially if you have already jumped to a different input field. Add a command so that the contents of the input buffer can be flushed.

11. Write an input subroutine that will print formatted numbers (as in program NUMFORM, Section 1.17), without the use of PRINT USING. The program must accept double-precision numbers and handle both the decimal point and the negative sign. You can have the prompt line when the field is empty, but as soon as a number, sign, or decimal point enters, you must print one integer digit, the decimal point, and the number of decimal digits you decide. Since only one number enters every time, apart from the Ctrl-H's and other cursor movement, you will need to print only one character.

12. Up to now, we have been rejecting control characters, or accepting them only when they have a special purpose. Modify an input subroutine so that after a certain command you can enter a letter which will be converted to the corresponding control character. (Thus, ''A'' will enter as Ctrl-A after the command.)

OUTPUT

2

Just as important as controlling the input is showing the information processed by the program in a way that is clear and easy to understand. It is therefore necessary to have control over the length and position of every number and string PRINTed.

Constants are not usually a problem, since their length can always be known in advance. Here are two examples of constants whose length will never vary:

PRINT 345.1

PRINT"The sun is shining".

With variables, the great range of possibilities makes control of the output more complicated. Strings can have from 0 to 255 characters, and numbers from 1 (e.g., 3, 8) to 22 (e.g., $-6.832760995100521D+18$).

The command PRINT USING is a tremendously powerful tool for control of the output, and a few extra notes or remarks can make its use optimal. This chapter will bring forth some of these notes or remarks and discuss some situations that can lead to errors or confusing output of numbers and strings. It will also provide some methods to prevent or correct those situations.

2.1 PRINT USING
FORMAT SPECIFICATION

The format specification part of the PRINT USING command can be either a string constant or a variable. Use of a variable allows greater flexibility, since the format can be changed between PRINTs, and the same command can produce a variety of results. Besides the formats described in the manual of BASIC-80 and in coming sections, the format field can contain literals (the characters contained in a pair of quotes or in a string variable) before and after the formatting symbols. As an example, Program Fragment 2.1 will print:

```
The rate today is 5.80 lower than yesterday

10 A=5.8
20 PRINT USING"The rate today is ##.## lower than yesterday";A
```

Program Fragment 2.1

String expressions can also be used in the format. If Program Fragment 2.2 is executed and answered with "Gabriel", the output will be:

```
Good morning, Gabriel.  How are you ?".
10 START$="Good morning, ":ENDING$=". How are you ?"
20 INPUT"Your name ";NAME$
30 PRINT USING START$+"&"+ENDING$;NAME$
```

Program Fragment 2.2

Line 30 could be changed to

30 PRINT START + NAME$ + ENDINGS$

but the PRINT USING offers more control.

PRINTING FIELD

After the format specification field, one or more expressions, separated by semicolons, specify the elements to print. They can be strings or numbers, constants, variables, or expressions. The formats are strictly of numerical or string type, mutually exclusive, so that the two cannot be combined with the same formatting field. If more than one expression is to be PRINTed, they must be separated by semicolons. The last expression can be followed by a comma or a semicolon. Since anything following a semicolon is interpreted as an expression that must be PRINTed, only expressions of the same type as the one specified by the formatting field can be used. The line

10 PRINT USING"###,.##";VALUE;A$

produces a 'type mismatch' error because A$ is not of numeric type and therefore cannot be processed by the numeric formatting field. If you want to attach a string at the end of a numeric PRINT USING, a new PRINT command must be used.

2.2 FORMATTING STRINGS

Three different formatting field modes are allowed for strings:

" \ n spaces \ " The field will PRINT n + 2 characters. If more are available in the string expression, the rest will be chopped off. If the expression has fewer than n + 2 characters, the rest will be filled with spaces. The following three lines produce the same output. The first is shortest and fastest, but the other two put the printing field into a variable, allowing more control from within the program.

PRINT USING" \ n spaces \ ";B$

A$ = SPACES$(N + 2):LSET A$ = B$:PRINT A$

A$ = LEFT$(B$ + SPACE$(N + 2),N + 2):PRINT A$

"!" Only the first character of the print field will be PRINTed. This format is included because the smallest format attainable with the backslashes is two characters (" \ \ ").

"&" PRINTs the string expression exactly as it is.

2.3 FORMATTING NUMBERS

The basic formatting element in numeric fields is the number sign (#) used to specify the number of digits on each side of the decimal point. If the value of the numeric expression is less than 1, a zero is provided as the only integer digit (unless the decimal point is the first character in the format field). If there is a decimal point, the number of decimal digits specified by the number of "#"'s is PRINTed; if there are fewer, zeros are provided; if there are more, the digits that are truncated are used to round the number up or down. (If the first decimal digit not PRINTed is greater or equal to five, the number is rounded up; otherwise, it is rounded down.) If there are not enough integer digits to fill the fields to the left of the decimal point, spaces are provided to produce the length specified. This length is kept constant to facilitate the alignment of numbers on the decimal point. The only circumstance in which the length is not kept constant is when there are more integer digits than the format specifies, in which case all the digits are printed, and the field is preceded by a percent sign (%).

A comma placed anywhere to the left of the decimal point makes the format add commas every three integer digits.

Two dollar signs at the beginning of the numeric format field make the number be PRINTed with a dollar sign to the left of the first integer digit.

A double asterisk at the beginning of the format field makes all the leading spaces be filled with asterisks.

Four up-arrows (∧) make the number be PRINTed in exponential form. The decimal point can be placed anywhere in the format field. The format will be respected, and the exponent adjusted to reflect the shift of the decimal point.

A plus sign at the beginning or end of the format field will make the number be PRINTed with the appropriate sign before or after it, in the position specified. (If the plus sign is omitted, only the negative sign [and, of course, the space for it] will be provided.)

A minus sign at the end of the format field causes negative numbers to be PRINTed with a trailing minus sign.

2.4 ROUNDING

PRINT USING rounds the digits that are left out of the formatted output. It is a very convenient feature, but it can lead to some confusion and inaccuracy. Consider the following example. Based on information about the employees of a company, a program must calculate the payment of overtime using a formula that will produce many decimal digits. When the number is PRINTED, these invisible digits are used to round the number up or down, and the result is very close to the actual figure. Unfortunately, when the total of these numbers is calculated, the digits that are not displayed add up to a number which, though very close to the value of the number printed, is not necessarily exact. Although the difference might be as small as a few pennies, most situations require a perfectly accurate figure without showing tenths or hundredths of a penny.

The way to solve this problem is to round the numbers up or down before they are treated by the PRINT USING format, so that no significant invisible decimal digits are left. Two methods will be discussed here: rounding up to the nearest integer number; and rounding decimal digits greater than or equal to five upwards, and those less than five downwards. The second method is usually called 'rounding up fives.'

INTEGER ROUND

Let's suppose you want to do the output in integer numbers only. If your intermediate calculations yield at least a hundredth (the equivalent of a penny in currency), you want to round up to the nearest integer. Citing the analogy of the dollar and cents, if you have even one cent in your number, you should add one dollar to the total. Only when the number is an integer do you leave it as it is. This is achieved if you add 0.99 to the number and take the integer part. Here are two examples:

$$N = 123.75$$
$$N = N + .99 \quad (N = 124.74)$$
$$N = INT(N) \quad (N = 124)$$

$$N = 500.02$$
$$N = N + .99 \quad (N = 501.01)$$
$$N = INT(N) \quad (N = 501)$$

Function 2.1 accepts a single-precision number and returns it rounded up to the nearest integer. Function 2.2 does the same with double-precision values.

```
10 DEF FN INT.ROUND(X)=INT(X+.99)
```

Function 2.1 Single-precision integer round

```
10 DEF FN INT.ROUND#(X#)=INT(X#+.99)
```

Function 2.2 Double-precision integer round

ROUND UP FIVES

The usual way to round numbers (mostly in calculations that deal with currency) is to add 0.005 (half a penny) to the value and take the integer part. Let's look at two examples:

$$N = 33.5015$$
$$N = N*100 \quad (N = 3350.15)$$
$$N = N + .5 \quad (N = 3350.65)$$
$$N = INT(N) \quad (N = 3350)$$
$$N = N/100 \quad (N = 33.50)$$

$$N = 47.376$$
$$N = N*100 \quad (N = 4737.6)$$
$$N = N + .5 \quad (N = 4738.1)$$

$$N = INT(N) \qquad (N = 4738)$$
$$N = N/100 \qquad (N = 47.38)$$

This method can be generalized as follows. Multiply the number by a power of ten, so that the last significant digit becomes the smallest integer. Then add 0.5, take the integer part, and divide by the same power of ten which you used to multiply. In the example, the last significant digit was a penny, or a hundredth, so we multiplied by 100, or 10^2, added 0.5, got the integer part, and divided by 100. In the next example, we choose to have only one decimal place:

$$N = 8.178$$
$$N = N*10^1 \qquad (N = 81.78)$$
$$N = N + 0.5 \qquad (N = 82.28)$$
$$N = INT(N) \qquad (N = 82)$$
$$N = N/10^1 \qquad (N = 8.2)$$

2.5 FAST SCREEN DRAWING

In this section we look at a technique to create screens very rapidly with a minimum number of instructions.

Most of the video terminals of today support a wide variety of features, such as cursor movement in the four directions[1], different attributes (inverse, flash), and even orthogonal graphics. (In this mode some characters become junctions—horizontal and vertical lines— that you can combine to make frames and do limited graphics.) The following examples will use the three nondestructive cursor movements available on most terminals: left (backspace), down (line feed), and left margin (carriage return). Cursor-right will be simulated with the space. To move the cursor up, use the sequence carriage return, Ctrl-H. (Return to the left margin of the current line and backspace, leaving the cursor at the right margin of the previous line.)

Suppose you want to draw the frame shown in Figure 2.1:

Figure 2.1

---

[1]Up, down, left and right; this is different from direct cursor addressing, which can position the cursor anywhere on the screen.

Since most terminals support an addressable cursor (i.e., a cursor that you can position anywhere on the screen), you could use the cursor to start at the top left corner, draw the plus sign, the line of hyphens and the final plus sign, calculate the vertical and horizontal position of the first exclamation mark, send the cursor there and print the "¦", do the same in the following lines, and print the final line sending the cursor to the beginning of the line. This requires many instructions, time, and space, but is the most commonly used technique.

An alternative way would be to have every line in a string stored in a file or as DATA, and PRINT them in sequence. Since every line must have at least the length of the rightmost character (unless TABs are used, but the savings are not great), a lot of space is wasted.

A third way, the fastest and most economical of the three, is to use the cursor-movement characters in sequence to draw the entire frame with a single PRINT command. (In this section we will only do the echo to show how to create the screen; later we will store the input for later use.) Program Fragment 2.3 echoes the characters as they are typed, to let you visualize the process. The cursor can be moved down by pressing Ctrl-J (line feed); use it to put the cursor in the line where you want the first row of hyphens. To move the cursor to the next position of the first plus sign, use either spaces or TAB (Ctrl-I), and type the line. To move the cursor to the next line down, type a line feed and a carriage return; the cursor should now be in the left margin of the next line, from where you can move it to get to the position of the first "¦". Repeat the process to draw the other "¦"'s. Now, you have several alternatives to draw the bottom line: (1) draw the plus sign, backspace to the beginning of the line, and draw the plus sign and the hyphens; (2) enter two backspaces, print the hyphen, enter two more backspaces, print the hyphen, etc., which is obviously less efficient, but which allows you to do the line step by step; and (3) PRINT a carriage return (CHR$(13)) to move the cursor to the left margin of the screen, and repeat the process of the top line.

```
10 HOME
20 W$=INPUT$(1)
30 PRINT W$;:GOTO 20
40 GOTO 20
```

Program Fragment 2.3

As you can see, to get around on the screen in a very fast way, we are using the special control characters that we rejected in Chapter 1. Now we are going to store the characters in a string variable, so that the entire figure can be drawn with a single PRINT command.

Program FASTSCRE adds a few convenient features. If you type Ctrl-E, a hyphen is printed to the left of the cursor, which is moved by printing two Ctrl-H's. If esc is typed, the cursor is moved to the next line and previous position. Since return is a powerful character here (to move the cursor to the left of the line), it cannot be used to signal the end of the input. Ctrl-K will be used instead.

Since this is only a demonstration program, the length of X$ (the variable in which the characters are stored) is not controlled, so that if more than 255 characters are entered, a 'string too long' error will halt the process. Perhaps the easiest way to control the length is by means of an ON ERROR GOTO command. Since only 255 characters can be processed, the screens that can be drawn with this program are limited, but they can show you how to use some of the capabilities of the system in a very efficient way. In the next section, a more elaborate program will be presented.

If you exploit all the capabilities of your terminal with this method, you can accelerate the creation of screens to near-machine speed. For example, if your terminal has a character or a sequence of characters to erase the screen, adding it at the beginning of your string will economize one instruction.

```
O '
                    ** FASTSCRE **
             Fast screen drawing

5 HOME:CTRL.H$=CHR$(8):BS$=CTRL.H$+"-"+CTRL.H$:
  ESC$=CHR$(27):CTRL.D$=CHR$(4):CTRL.J$=CHR$(10):
  CTRL.K$=CHR$(11)
10 W$=INPUT$(1):
   IF W$=ESC$
     THEN
        PRINT BS$;:X$=X$+BS$:GOTO 10
15 IF W$=CTRL.D$
     THEN
        PRINT CTRL.H$;CTRL.J$;:
        X$=X$+CTRL.H$+CTRL.J$:GOTO 10
20 IF W$<>CTRL.K$
     THEN
        PRINT W$;:X$=X$+W$:GOTO 10
     ELSE
        HOME:PRINT X$;:GOTO 10
```

Program 2.1

2.6 FAST SCREEN EDITOR

We will use the method explained in the previous section to develop an editor. This will allow you to use the fast-screen sequences of characters in your programs.

The two main limitations of program FASTSCRE were that only 255 characters were allowed and that the sequence could not be permanently stored for later use. To solve the first problem, we will use an array instead of a single string variable. As an added convenience, a command will be added to erase the last character typed.

Program FASTSCED uses the array SCR$ to store the characters. SCR$ is DIMensioned to accept ten strings, which means that up to 2550 characters can be processed. If more are needed, a bigger DIM can be used, but with more characters the screen is so full that it is easier to use the entire lines and not to bother with fancy cursor movements. When a character or a sequence of characters must be stored, the subroutine starting on line 200 checks the length of SCR$(I), the current line. If the addition of X$ (the characters to add) results in a length greater than 255, the index I is incremented, and X$ added to the next line.

To erase the last character (Ctrl-E has been chosen as the command to backspace), we cannot use the techniques used in the input subroutines of Chapter 1, since the previous cursor position cannot easily be determined. We could analyze the previous character and perform complicated movements to get to the previous position, but it is not worth the effort. An easier way is to delete the last character in SCR$(I) and redraw the entire screen. When line 20 detects Ctrl-E, it checks the length of SCR$(I). If SCR$(I) has no characters, I must be decremented (providing it is greater than 1), and the last character of the previous SCR$ must be deleted. If the length of SCR$(I) is at least 1, the rightmost character is deleted. In both cases the screen must be redrawn. (Subroutine 300 PRINTs SCR$ up to the current value of N.)

Saving SCR$ on disk is not as easy as it might seem at first sight. If it is sent as a sequential file, the control characters in SCR$ might (and very often will) have unexpected effects. Control characters or sequences of them are used to indicate the end of the file or to delimit items. Since random sequences are produced by the program, it is often the case that the file cannot be read back as written. The easiest way to ensure that what is saved is retrieved faithfully is to store the ASCII code of every character and convert it back to its original form with the CHR$ function. Ctrl-K is used to go to a small menu with four options: SAVE, LOAD, CONTINUE, and END. When line 10 detects a Ctrl-K, the program jumps to line 400, the menu. Line 500 SAVEs the file in the way described above, and line 550 LOADs it.

More economical and faster ways to save SCR$ on disk will be explained in Chapter 4.

```
O
                    ** FASTSCED **
                Fast screen with edition

5 HOME:CTRL.H$=CHR$(8):BS$=CTRL.H$+"-"+CTRL.H$:
  ESC$=CHR$(27):CTRL.K$=CHR$(11):CTRL.D$=CHR$(4):
  CTRL.E$=CHR$(5):DIM SCR$(10):J=1:N=1:
  WIDTH(255):LINE.FEED$=CHR$(10)
10 W$=INPUT$(1):
   IF W$=CTRL.K$
     THEN
       400
15 IF W$=ESC$
     THEN
       X$=BS$:GOSUB 200:PRINT X$;:GOTO 10
17 IF W$=CTRL.D$
     THEN
       X$=CTRL.H$+LINE.FEED$:GOSUB 200:PRINT X$;:
       GOTO 10
20 IF W$=CTRL.E$
     THEN
       IF LEN(SCR$(N))>1
         THEN
           HOME:
           SCR$(N)=LEFT$(SCR$(N),LEN(SCR$(N))-1):
           GOSUB 300:GOTO 10
         ELSE
           IF N>1
             THEN
               SCR$(N)="":N=N-1:GOSUB 200:GOTO 10
             ELSE
               10
50 X$=W$:GOSUB 200:PRINT X$;:GOTO 10
100 HOME:
    FOR I%=1 TO N:
      PRINT SCR$(I%);:
    NEXT:
    RETURN
110 GOTO 110
200 IF LEN(SCR$(N))+LEN(X$)>255
      THEN
        N=N+1
210 SCR$(N)=SCR$(N)+X$:
    RETURN
300 HOME:
    FOR I=1 TO N:
      PRINT SCR$(I);:
    NEXT:
    RETURN
400 HOME:PRINT"1-SAVE":PRINT"2-LOAD":
    PRINT"3-CONTINUE":PRINT"4-END ";
410 W$=INPUT$(1):
    IF W$<"1"OR W$>"4"
      THEN
        410
```

```
        ELSE
           PRINT:ON VAL(W$) GOTO 500,550,600,650
500  INPUT"FILENAME: ";FL.NAME$:
     OPEN"O",1,FL.NAME$:
     FOR I=1 TO N:
        FOR J=1 TO LEN(SCR$(I)):
           PRINT#1,ASC(MID$(SCR$(I),J,1)):
        NEXT
510  NEXT:CLOSE:GOSUB 300:GOTO 10
550  INPUT"FILENAME: ";FL.NAME$:
     FOR I=1 TO 10:
        SCR$(I)="":
     NEXT:I=1:
     OPEN"I",1,FL.NAME$:
     WHILE NOT EOF(1):
        INPUT#1,TEMP:
        SCR$(I)=SCR$(I)+CHR$(TEMP)
560     IF LEN(SCR$(I))=255
           THEN
              I=I+1
570  WEND:CLOSE:N=I:GOSUB 300:GOTO 10
600  GOSUB 300:GOTO 10
650  END
```

Program 2.2

2.7 REDIRECTING THE OUTPUT

In Section 1.18 we saw how to get input from a file instead of the keyboard. It is also very useful to be able to redirect the output. In most microcomputers, three devices—the screen, the disk, and the printer—can be used for output, and there are two ways to do the output: (1) send the stream of characters followed by a carriage return—line feed (the equivalent of executing a PRINT without a final semicolon); or (2) send the characters as they are (which means that the next characters will be appended to the ones just written).

Subroutine 1000 of program REDIRECT uses the value in the variable DEST to decide between the seven different output combinations:

1 PRINT

2 LPRINT

3 PRINT # (TO A FILE)

4 PRINT and LPRINT

5 PRINT and PRINT #

6 LPRINT and PRINT #

7 PRINT, LPRINT, and PRINT #

If, instead of using PRINT commands, you send the string to be printed to BUFF\$ (the temporary buffer), the redirect subroutine will PRINT it according to the destination specified in DEST. If BUFF\$ is sent to subroutine 10010, it will be PRINTed as if followed by a semicolon (not followed by a carriage return—line feed). If it is sent to line 10000, there are two possibilities when trying to end BUFF\$ with a carriage return–line feed: (1) If BUFF\$ has fewer than 254 characters, the carriage return and line feed can be added at the end of BUFF\$, and the subroutine continued. (2) If BUFF\$ is too long to accept two extra characters, it is PRINTed by subroutine 10010. On RETURN from the subroutine (still at line 10000), a carriage return and line feed are placed in BUFF\$ (erasing its previous contents) and sent to subroutine 10010.

Although the redirect subroutine is used in a very elementary way in this program, it can give you an idea of how easy it is to choose the destination of your output. This is an easy way to get hard copies of your output,[2] but a special note should be made: most printers do not move the head back with a Ctrl-H and if they do, two or more letters will overlap. To resolve this difficulty, you can make your program wait until your input is completed to echo it in the printer or disk. The redirect subroutine is very handy to get a disk copy of your working session, which can later be analyzed in case of an error. You can also check what is being sent to the disk by printing it on the screen. When you do not need to see it anymore, simply change the value of DEST.

o

```
            ** REDIRECT **
            Redirect output

5 CR.RET$=CHR$(13):LINE.FEED$=CHR$(10)
10 HOME:INPUT"FILENAME: ";FILE.NAME$:
    INPUT"BUFFER # ";FILE:
    IF FILE.NAME$<>""
      THEN
        OPEN"O",FILE,FILE.NAME$
15 PRINT"DESTINATION ? ":
    PRINT"1- PRINT":
    PRINT"2- LPRINT":
    PRINT"3- PRINT#1":
    PRINT"4- PRINT AND LPRINT":
    PRINT"5- PRINT AND PRINT#1":
    PRINT"6- LPRINT AND PRINT#1":
```

---

[2]You can have a copy of what comes out on the screen as well as of what you enter in the keyboard if you echo the characters of the input subroutine using subroutine 10000 instead of a PRINT command.

```
      PRINT"7- PRINT, LPRINT AND PRINT#1 ";:
      INPUT DEST
   20 LINE INPUT BUFF$:GOSUB 10000:GOTO 20
   10000 IF LEN(BUFF$)<254
         THEN
            BUFF$=BUFF$+CR.RET$+LINE.FEED$
         ELSE
            GOSUB 10000:BUFF$=CR.RET$+LINE.FEED$
   10010 ON DEST GOTO 10020,10030,10040,
                      10050,10060,10070,10080
   10020 PRINT BUFF$;:RETURN
   10030 PRINT#FILE,BUFF$;:RETURN
   10040 LPRINT BUFF$;:RETURN
   10050 PRINT BUFF$;:PRINT#FILE,BUFF$;:RETURN
   10060 PRINT BUFF$;:LPRINT BUFF$;:RETURN
   10070 LPRINT BUFF$;:PRINT#FILE,BUFF$;:RETURN
   10080 PRINT BUFF$;:LPRINT BUFF$;:
         PRINT#FILE,BUFF$;:RETURN
```

Program 2.3

2.8 PRINT USING IN STRING VARIABLES

The convenience of the PRINT USING instruction is limited by the fact that it can only be used in PRINT commands, and the resulting string is not available to the program. (It is only available for "export," never locally.)

After a file is OPENed for random access and FIELDed, there are two ways to transfer data to the corresponding buffer before executing the PUT statement that sends it to disk. One, the most frequently used, is by means of LSET or RSET; the other is PRINT# or PRINT USING#. With this second method, the stream of characters is placed in the file buffer as shown in Figure 2.2. If the first fielded variable is at least as long as what was PRINTed in the buffer, the characters can be copied into a string variable, gaining access to the PRINT USING formats from within the program.

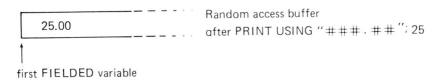

Figure 2.2

If a second PRINT or PRINT USING is directed to the buffer, the output is done as in a sequential file, and the characters of this second PRINT will follow those of the first one, as shown in Figure 2.3.[3] It is better to use the first field of the buffer to access the output with PRINT USING. A GET # buffer ,1 sets the file pointer to the beginning of the buffer, so that the next PRINT can be accessed through the first FIELDed variable.

```
┌─────────────────────── ─ ─ ─ ─
│  25.00    0.10                   Buffer after second
└─────────────────────── ─ ─ ─ ─  PRINT USING " ###.##"; 0.1
```

Figure 2.3

Program PRINUSI gives you access to the formatted output in B$ on line 50. Notice that the length of the resulting field (how many spaces the PRINTed field will occupy) must be known in advance, or the access to the buffer will not correspond to the length of the output. This length can be calculated using Program Fragment 1.2. Since any number of FIELD statements can be active simultaneously, any number of formats can be accessed using this method.

```
O

                    ** PRINUSI **
            PRINT USING in string variable.

10 OPEN"R",1,"WKFL"
20 FIELD#1,12 AS A$:LSET A$=SPACE$(20)
25 INPUT W#
30 PRINT#1,USING"$$#######,.##";W#
40 B$=A$
50 PRINT B$
60 GET 1,1:GOTO 25
```

Program 2.4

2.9 OUTPUT IN FIELDS OF FIXED LENGTH

In the production of comprehensible reports, it is essential that the columns of numbers be aligned on the decimal point. Compare columns a and b in Figure 2.4 to see the difference.

---

[3]When several PRINTs to the buffer attempt to place more characters than the buffer can take, a 'field overflow error' will make the program fail.

123.55	123.55
142	142.00
3	3.00
1,467.2	1,467.20
a	b

Figure 2.4

When the value formatted by PRINT USING has more integer digits than fields specified in the format, a percent sign is printed as the first character of the number, and then all the digits follow, as shown in Figure 2.5. This can mess up a printout completely. It can even make the line too long for the printer or the screen and have the final characters end up on the next line.

PRINT USING "# # #";1492

Actually Prints:

%1492

Figure 2.5

You can try to prevent this kind of problem by using controlled input for all your numbers, checking lengths frequently, or using other techniques. But an easier way (and closer to failproof) is to PRINT the number USING the required format with the method described in Section 2.8, get it in a string variable, and examine it. In program USINGTST, line 6020 checks the leftmost character of B$. If its first character is a percent sign, the number of digits exceeded the format fields, and B$ is filled with 'greater than' ("□") signs, so that when B$ is actually sent to the screen or the printer, it shows that there is something wrong with the number in it, but the rest of the report is not affected. B$ must, of course, have the same length as the formatted number.

```
10 '
                      ** USINGTST **
              Check length with PRINT USING

20 OPEN"R",1,"WKFL":FIELD#1,12 AS A$:LSET A$=SPACE$(20)
25 INPUT W#
6000 '
              Format number, check length

6010 PRINT#1,USING"$$#######,.##";W#:B$=A$
6020 IF LEFT$(B$,1)="%"
```

```
      THEN
          B$=STRING$(12,">")
6030  GET  1,1:RETURN
```

Program 2.5

Exercises

1. In Program 2.2, when your screen has many characters, and you want to delete more than one, you have to wait until all of SCR$ is printed again. Modify the program so that the last character can be deleted without waiting for the screen update. (Use INKEY$ while updating the screen.)

2. The format specification part of PRINT USING accepts up to 24 number signs for numeric formatting, but numbers with more than 16 digits can only be correctly formatted in exponential form. Write a subroutine that accepts any number (with positive and negative exponents) and prints it in nonexponential form, as shown in Figure 2.6.

1.8765E + 23 and 7.34576123D + 18 will be printed as

18765000000000000000000   and
7345761230000000000.

5.34861E – 13 and – 9.13243557D – 21 will be printed as

0.00000000000534861   and
– 0.00000000000000000000913243557

Figure 2.6 Very small and large numbers.

3. Write a program that will simulate a clock on the screen. (Don't be concerned with accuracy.) Suppose that a duplicate of this clock is being used in a public place and the screen can never be disturbed. Use the printer as a local terminal to change the hour or the date.

4. Write a subroutine to redirect the output so that you can at any moment get in the printer a copy of the current state of the screen. Use an array of 24 strings, one for each line, to store every change in the screen. The copy can then be made directly from this array.

5. Modify program FASTSCRE to store the characters (in ASCII form) in an array of integers.

6. Write two programs that redirect output and input such that the output of the first program is used as the input of the second one.

HANDLING DATA

3

One of the most frequent uses of computers today is to handle collections of data—to store and retrieve information in a fast and efficient way. Because of the constantly decreasing cost in the storage units (diskettes, hard disks, tapes) and central memory, greater and greater amounts of information can be stored in the small- and medium-sized computers. As the size of the collection of data grows, so does the complexity of its manageability, and even an impeccable collection is useless if the search for, insertion, modification, and deletion of an item take too long. What good is a big library if you do not have a system to find a book, and you must spend days looking for it? Or imagine looking for a number in a telephone book which is not in alphabetical order!

Even in programs in which the main goal is not to store data, but to perform calculations, you will find that you must store and retrieve relatively large collections of numbers that are related in some way, numbers that must be handled efficiently. That the problem of data handling is important is evidenced by the fact that about seventy percent of all computing time is spent sorting.[1]

There are many ways to store and handle information in a computer, some better for some situations that others, but there is no

---

[1]To *sort* is to put the elements of a collection in order. When numbers are sorted, the order is from smaller to bigger; when strings are sorted, the order is the usual lexicographic order.

single method faster and more economical in memory requirements than the rest. The choice of method depends on the particular application.

In this chapter, we discuss some common methods of handling information and examine the circumstances in which they perform better than others.

3.1 SHUTTLE SORT

The shuttle sort is one of the simplest methods of sorting and one of the most inefficient, yet, it is very simple and the algorithm is but a few lines long. When you have to sort a small number of elements in a hurry, the shuttle sort will most likely be the only sorting method you will remember.

Before trying to understand the shuttle sort, let's study a method of finding the smallest element in an array. We shall store in the array M% a collection of 100 random numbers. We want to find the smallest one and interchange it with the number in the first position of the array. Line 20 of program SMALLEST assumes that the smallest number is in position M%(1) and, using I% as an index, compares it with M%(2). If M%(2) is smaller than M%(1), the two numbers are SWAPped. (This way, the two numbers change position but are still intact.) Then M%(1) is compared with M%(3), and SWAPped if necessary. The process is repeated for every M%(I), so that at the end we can be sure that the value in M%(1) is the smallest of the entire array.

```
10 '
                        ** SMALLEST **
               Find the smallest of 100 numbers

20 HOME:RANDOMIZE
30 N=100:DIM M%(N):
   FOR I=1 TO N:
     M%(I)=INT(1000*RND):
   NEXT
40 I=1:
   FOR J=2 TO N:
     IF M%(I)>M%(J)
       THEN
         SWAP M%(I),M%(J)
50 NEXT
60 FOR I=1 TO N:
     PRINT M%(I);:
   NEXT
```

Program 3.1

To sort all the numbers in an array of N elements, we find the smallest and place it in M%(1). Then we find the smallest of the remaining array, from 2 to N, and place it in M%(2). The third time, the smallest from M%(3) to M%(N) will be left in M%(3). The process is repeated until the array goes from M%(N − 1) to M%(N), which leaves the last two elements in order. Figure 3.1 shows a shuttle sort with four elements. The numbers in the circles indicate the comparisons.

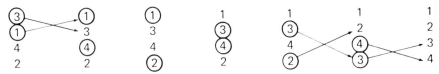

Figure 3.1 Shuttle sort

In program shuttle, line 10 asks for the size of the array and fills it with random integer numbers from 0 to 999. Line 20 starts a FOR loop that will use I% to indicate the beginning of the subarray. The first time, when I% = 1, the smallest number from 1 to N will be found and placed in M%(1). The second time, when I% = 2, the smallest from 2 to N will be placed in M%(2), etc. Notice that I% only needs to go to N − 1, because then the smallest from N − 1 to N will be placed in M%(N − 1), and there will be only one number left, M%(N), which will be the largest of the array.

When I% = 1, the second FOR loop of line 20 will use J% to compare M%(1) with M%(2), with M%(3), etc. In other words, the job of the J% loop will be to find the smallest number from M%(I) to M%(N).

```
  1  '
                    ** SHUTTLE **
                    Shuttle sort.

  5   HOME
 10   INPUT"NUMBER OF ITEMS TO SORT:";N:DIM M%(N):
      FOR I%=1 TO N:
        M%(I%)=INT(1000*RND):
      NEXT
 20   FOR I%=1 TO N-1:
        FOR J%=I%+1 TO N:
          IF M%(I%)>M%(J%)
            THEN
              SWAP M%(I%),M%(J%)
 40     NEXT:
        PRINT CHR$(13);I%;:
      NEXT
```

```
50 PRINT:
   FOR I% = 1 TO N:
      PRINT M%(I%);:
   NEXT
```

Program 3.2

If you want to sort strings instead of numbers, simply replace every occurrence of M% by M$. Comparisons between strings are done according to lexicographic order and therefore produce the desired effect.

3.2 SPECIAL NOTES ON SORTING

When numbers are sorted, there are only two possibilities: the order can be by ascending value or descending value. When strings are sorted (strings can be compared using the relational operators =, >, <, >=, etc.), the same comparisons can be made as for numbers, but several points must be considered:

If numbers in string form are sorted, the final order will correspond to the numerical sequence only if all the strings have the same length. (Thus, "123" is smaller than "124", but "001" is greater than " 12", and "012" is smaller than "1".)

Lowercase letters come after uppercase ("a" is greater than "A"), and therefore "peter" comes after "Peter", and "alice" comes after "Zoo". If strict letter order is required, all strings must be set to a common mode, either uppercase or lowercase, using the method described in Section 1.16. However, if the contents of the strings must be preserved in their original form, the conversion can be made every time there is a comparison (which is tremendously inefficient), or a parallel array can be used to store the strings in common form. This multiplies by two the number of interchanges and therefore delays the process. To keep this number constant, use the method explained in Section 3.6.

If the record number of a random file is considered to be the index of an array, sorting on disk is nearly as easy as in memory. However, the process is slow. Methods to sort on disk are explained in Sections 3.5 and 3.9.

3.3 BINARY SEARCH

The biggest convenience of having the information sorted is that searching for a particular item can be done very efficiently. Think of the way you look for a name in the telephone book. You pick a page where you think the first letter of the name is and use it to partition the book in two. If you find that the page is right, you look for the name; if the name should be before that page, you do not have to bother with the second part of the book. You repeat the process with the corresponding part until you either find the name or see that it is not in the book. This same method is used in what is called a binary search.

Figure 3.2 shows a sorted array in which we are trying to find the number 68. The arrows show the part of the array under consideration. The circle indicates the number that is compared with 68. On the first pass we look in the middle of the two arrows (there are ten elements, so we look at position number five) and find 89 there. Since 68 is smaller than 89, we move the second arrow to the position before 89 to indicate that we are no longer interested in the numbers below this pointer. In this new situation, the array being considered goes from 1 to 71. We look in the middle and find a 67 there, which is smaller than our 68, so we move the first arrow up. On the third pass, the number in the center is 68, our number. Notice that only three passes were required. If the numbers were not sorted, we might have had to perform ten passes.

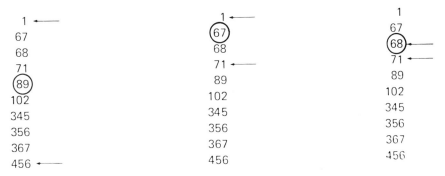

Figure 3.2 Successful search

Now we are going to look for the number 110 in the same list. (See Figure 3.3.) On the first pass, since 110 is greater than 89, we move the first arrow to position 6. The middle number is now 356, greater than 110, so we move the second arrow to position 7. The new center is 102, smaller than 110, and we move the first arrow to position 7. The new center is 345, larger than 110, so we move the second arrow to position 6. Since the first arrow is now in a position greater than the second one, there are no elements to study, and we can infer that the number 110 is not in the list. In this case four passes were necessary.

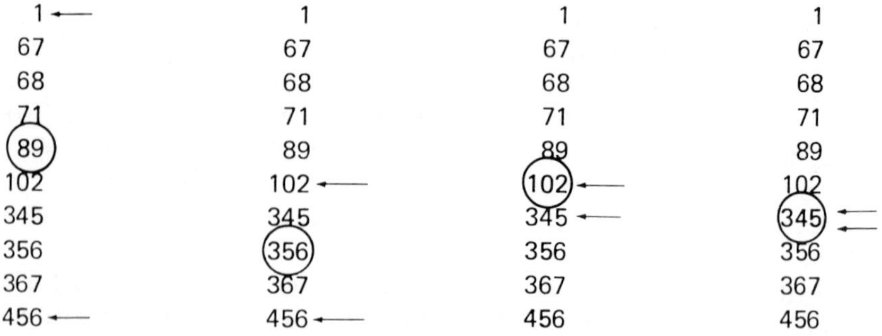

1 ←	1	1	1
67	67	67	67
68	68	68	68
71	71	71	71
(89)	89	89	89
102	102 ←	(102) ←	102
345	345	345 ←	(345) ⇇
356	(356)	356	356
367	367	367	367
456 ←	456 ←	456	456

Figure 3.3 Failed search

It can be proven that in the worst case the maximum number of comparisons made is roughly equivalent to LOG(N) (the actual figure is log base two of N, plus one), where N is the number of items in the list. This means that if you have 1000 items, the program will have to do at the most 11 comparisons, as opposed to one thousand for an unsorted list. When the number is 10,000 the number of comparisons is 15 to ten thousand!

Program BSEARCH stores random numbers in the array M% and uses a shuttle sort in lines 20 to 40 to put them in order. SEARCH will contain the number to search for, and UPPER and LOWER will be used as the arrows in the previous examples. On the first pass, they are set to 1 and N to examine the entire array. If the while loop terminates at line 1050, the number has not been found, and line 1060 sets M to zero. Otherwise, M RETURNs with the index of M% pointing to the location of the number SEARCH.

```
0  '
                      ** BSEARCH **
                      Binary search

5 HOME
10 INPUT"Number of items ";N:DIM M(N):
      FOR I=1 TO N:
         M(I)=INT(1000*RND):
      NEXT
20 FOR I=1 TO N-1:
         FOR J=I+1 TO N
30       IF M(I)>M(J)
            THEN
               SWAP M(I),M(J)
40    NEXT:
         PRINT CHR$(13);I;:
      NEXT:PRINT
45 FOR I=1 TO N:
         PRINT I,M(I):
```

```
        NEXT
50 INPUT"Number to find ";SEARCH:GOSUB 1000:
    IF M<>0
        THEN
            PRINT"Found in position "M
        ELSE
            PRINT"Not found"
60 GOTO 45
1000 '
            ** Binary search subroutine **

1005 LOWER=1:UPPER=N
1010 WHILE LOWER<=UPPER:
        M=(LOWER+UPPER)\2
1020    IF M(M)=SEARCH
            THEN
                RETURN
1030    IF SEARCH>M(M)
            THEN
                LOWER=M+1:GOTO 1050
            ELSE
                UPPER=M-1
1050 WEND
1060 M=0:RETURN
```

Program 3.3

3.4 SHELL SORT

The technique used in the shell sort is completely different from the one described in the previous section: the program is short and much faster than the shuttle sort, but harder to understand.

Without going into too much detail, let's see an example on how it works. Figure 3.4a shows the array to be sorted, in its original form. Throughout the sort, we will use some GUIDE number to decide which numbers to compare. The initial GUIDE will be the largest power of two which is smaller than or equal to the number of elements in the array, minus one. In our example, $N = 8$, and since $2^3 = 8$, we choose 3 as our GUIDE. (The GUIDE will always be chosen from the sequence 1, 3, 7, 15, 31, etc.) In Figure 3.4, the circles show the number being compared, and the arrows indicate the interchanges. The first comparison (Figure 3.4a) is made between the first and fourth elements (the first and the first plus the GUIDE). The 15 and the 1 must be SWAPped. Since the 1 cannot sink any further, it stays in position number one. Figures 3.4b and 3.4c show comparisons without interchange. The comparison shown in part d makes the -3 and 15 be SWAPped. Since there is still room for the -3 to sink if it has to, it is compared with the number 1 as shown in Figure 3.4e. This comparison leaves the −3 at the first position of the array. Figure 3.4f shows another comparison that leads to an interchange: the 32 and the 5. In this case, the next comparison finds that the 5 does not have to sink anymore. Since no more couples can be analyzed with this GUIDE number, the next is found, viz., 1. Figures 3.4h and 3.4i show two comparisons that require no interchange. In Figure 3.4j, the 4 and the 1 are compared and SWAPped. The 1 is further compared with the 2 in Figure 3.4k and SWAPped with it. At this point the array is sorted, but there are still some more comparisons to make until the current GUIDE is exhausted. After this, since 1 is the smallest possible GUIDE number, the sort is terminated.

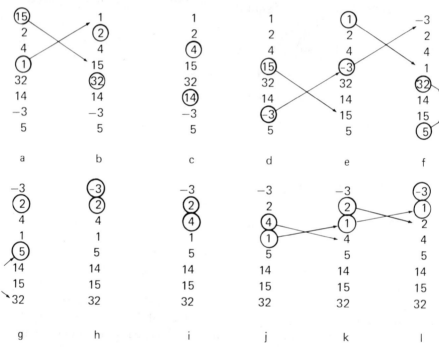

Figure 3.4 Sorting by means of the shell sort

The actual shell sort of program SHELL starts on line 1800 and ends on line 1850. To keep track of the advance of the program, line 1850 PRINTs the current GUIDE number. When it reaches zero, the sort is finished.

o ·

```
** SHELL **
Shell sort

10 HOME: INPUT "NUMBER OF ITEMS TO SORT: ";N%:
   DIM M%(N%)
```

```
 20 FOR I=1 TO N%:
       M%(I)=INT(1000*RND)▪
    NEXT
 30 GOSUB 1800:HOME:
    FOR I=1 TO N%:
      PRINT M%(I);:
    NEXT:
    END

1800 GUIDE%=1:'
            ** Shell sort subroutine **

1810 GUIDE%=2*GUIDE%:
      IF GUIDE%<N%
        THEN
          1810
        ELSE
          GUIDE%=(GUIDE%-1)\2
1820 WHILE GUIDE%>0:
        FOR I%=1 TO N%-GUIDE%:
          J%=I%
1840      WHILE J%>0:
            K%=J%+GUIDE%:
            IF M%(K%)<M%(J%)
              THEN
                SWAP M%(J%),M%(K%):J%=J%-GUIDE%:
          WEND
1850    NEXT:
        GUIDE%=(GUIDE%-1)\2:PRINT CHR$(13);GUIDE%;:
      WEND:
      RETURN
```

Program 3.4

3.5 TAGFILES

The two sorting methods studied so far, the shuttle sort and the shell sort, dealt with arrays of simple elements, either numbers or strings. Many times, though, this is not the case: what must be sorted is a collection of complex elements with two or more numbers or strings combined. An example of this would be data about a person that includes the person's name, social security number, address, telephone number, etc. In the previous sorting methods, when an element had to change position, it was physically moved by means of the SWAP instruction. This becomes impractical for items that are related to other entries which must be moved too.

If we add an extra array in which we keep the order of the collection of data, the sorting can be performed on this array without moving the actual data. Let's look at an example that will help us visualize the process. We shall sort an array of four numbers. Figure 3.5a shows the initial situation. The three columns in each shot are (from left to right) the actual index of the array, the tagfile, and the array that must be sorted. At the beginning, every element of the tagfile is equal to its index. The circles indicate the numbers involved in the comparison, but, unlike previous examples, the numbers at the end of the arrows will be compared, not the ones inside the circles. To look for the smallest element of the array (which must be recognizable as the first one), the first and second elements (11 and 23) are compared as shown in Figure 3.5a. Since there is no need for an interchange, the first and third elements are compared. There are still no movements; hence, the first and fourth elements are compared and are found to be in the wrong order. Instead of moving the actual numbers 11 and 7, the numbers in tagfile (1 and 4) are SWAPped. We have already found the smallest element of the array. Figure 3.5d shows the first comparison in the search for the second smallest number. There is no need for interchange. Figure 3.5e shows the comparison between the second and fourth elements, which must be SWAPped. Once more, it is the tagfile which is affected, and the result can be seen in Figure 3.5f. The last two elements (41 and 23) are compared, and Figure 3.5g shows the final situation. To read the elements in order, you could say "the first one is in position 4, the second one in position 1, the third one in position 2, and the last one in position 3."

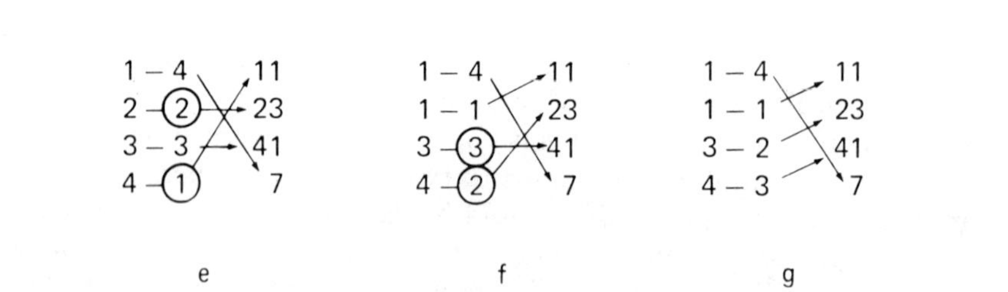

Figure 3.5 Shuttle sort with TAGFILE

Program TAGFILE sorts a collection of names and telephone numbers. TF% is used as tagfile, and is initialized with the numbers that correspond to its indices. Figure 3.6 shows the differences between the sort on lines 80–100 and a regular shuttle sort. Every time the sorted array is needed, the individual elements of the sorted arrays must be accessed through the TAGFILE.

TAGFILE	*SHUTTLE SORT*
IF N$(TF%(I%))>N$(TF%(J%))	IF N$(I%)>N$(J%)
SWAP TF%(I%),TF%(J%)	SWAP N$(I%),N$(J%)

Figure 3.6 Shuttle sort with and without TAGFILE

A shuttle sort was used for simplicity in this program, but a shell or insertion sort can be used as well.

Another convenient use of TAGFILES is to point to the record numbers of a random access file, so that there is no need to have the information in memory. The program can work with bigger collections of data, thus the size is limited by the capacity of the disk and the room for the TAGFILE. When an item is inserted or deleted, and the tagfile is re-sorted, only the key (see the explanation at the end of this section) must be brought to memory, since the information on the disk will not be moved.

```
0   ·
                        ** TAGFILE **
                 Bubble sort using tagfile

10 HOME:INPUT"Number of names :";N%:
   DIM N$(N%),TE$(N%),TF%(N%)
20 FOR I%=1 TO N%:
     TF%(I%)=I%:
   NEXT
30 FOR I%=1 TO N%:
     PRINT:INPUT"Name ";N$(I%):
     IF N$(I%)=""
       THEN
          80
       ELSE
          INPUT"Telephone ";TE$(I%)
70 NEXT
80 FOR I%=1 TO N%-1:
     FOR J%=I%+1 TO N%
90     IF N$(TF%(I%))  >  N$(TF%(J%))
         THEN
            SWAP TF%(I%),TF%(J%)
100   NEXT:
     NEXT
110 PRINT:
     FOR I%=1 TO N%:
       PRINT LEFT$(N$(TF%(I%))+
       STRING$(20," "),20)" "TE$(TF%(I%))" ":
     NEXT
```

Program 3.5

A *key* is the element used to decide the order. When an array of integers is sorted, the key is any of the integers. In the above example involving the names, telephone numbers, and social security numbers of a collection of people, one key can be the name (and the sort would be a string sort), another key can be the telephone number (numeric sort), and a third can be the social security number (numeric if the hyphens are omitted, string otherwise). Sometimes the key can be even shorter than the entire string. When sorting a collection of titles of books, for example, some names may be too long, and the sort would have to be made comparing strings of perhaps hundreds of characters. If you decide that only the first thirty characters will be used as the key, the sort will execute faster.

3.6 MULTIPLE TAGFILES

One of the biggest conveniences of the use of TAGFILEs is that the original information is not moved. When you have a collection of related items (such as name, telephone number, and social security number), you might want to access it by more than one key. However, since you usually have the information sorted in only one way, a binary search can be used with only one of the keys. If more than one TAGFILE is used, the information can be kept sorted by as many keys as the memory allows.

In program MULTAG, three arrays are used as TAGFILEs: TAG1, TAG2, and TAG3. Instruction 20 initializes the three to its indices, and lines 80–100 perform a simple shuttle sort. Line 90 sorts TAG1 using the name as key, line 93 sorts TAG2 using the telephone number, and line 96 sorts TAG3 using the social security number. Line 110 asks which key you want to use, and shows the information sorted, as indicated. Since the three sorted files are always kept in memory, a binary search can be done on any key.

Multiple TAGFILES can also be used for random access disk files.

```
O
                     ** MULTAG **
                   Multiple tagfile

10 HOME:INPUT"Number of persons : ";N%:
   DIM N$(N%),TE$(N%),SS$(N%),
       TAG1(N%),TAG2(N%),TAG3(N%)
20 FOR I%=1 TO N%:
       TAG1(I%)=I%:TAG2(I%)=I%:TAG3(I%)=I%:
       NEXT
30 FOR I%=1 TO N%:
       PRINT:INPUT"Name ";N$(I%):
       IF N$(I%)=""
```

```
          THEN
             80
          ELSE
             INPUT"Telephone ";TE$(I%):
             INPUT"Social security  ";SS$(I%)
 70 NEXT
 80 FOR I%=1 TO N%-1:
      FOR J%=I%+1 TO N%
 90    IF N$(TAG1(I%)) > N$(TAG1(J%))
             THEN
               SWAP TAG1(I%),TAG1(J%)
 92    IF TE$(TAG2(I%)) > TE$(TAG2(J%))
             THEN
               SWAP TAG2(I%),TAG2(J%)
 94    IF SS$(TAG3(I%)) > SS$(TAG3(J%))
             THEN
               SWAP TAG3(I%),TAG3(J%)
100   NEXT:
    NEXT
110 PRINT:PRINT"Print by:":PRINT"  1-Name":
    PRINT"  2-Telephone":
    PRINT"  3-Social security ";
120 W$=INPUT$(1):
    IF W$<"1"OR W$>"3"
        THEN
          120
        ELSE
          ON VAL(W$) GOTO 130,140,150
130 PRINT:
    FOR I%=1 TO N%:
      PRINT LEFT$(N$(TAG1(I%))+SPACE$(20),20)+
      TE$(TAG1(I%))"-"+
      LEFT$(SS$(TAG1(I%))+SPACE$(12),12):
    NEXT:GOTO 110
140 PRINT:
    FOR I%=1 TO N%:
      PRINT LEFT$(TE$(TAG2(I%))+SPACE$(8),8)" ";
      LEFT$(N$(TAG2(I%))+SPACE$(20),20)" "+
      LEFT$(SS$(TAG2(I%))+SPACE$(12),12):
    NEXT:GOTO 110
150 PRINT:
    FOR I%=1 TO N%:
      PRINT LEFT$(SS$(TAG3(I%))+SPACE$(12),12)" ";
      LEFT$(N$(TAG3(I%))+SPACE$(20),20)" "+
      LEFT$(TE$(TAG3(I%))+SPACE$(20),20):
    NEXT:GOTO 110
```

Program 3.6

3.7 INSERTION SORT

When you use either a shuttle or a shell sort, execution of the rest of the program has to await completion of the sort. There are many circumstances, however, in which data are entered item by item from the keyboard (as opposed to reading the entire array from a file, for example), and there is enough time between inputs to place the new entry at its appropriate location in the sorted file. Thus, an insertion sort sounds like an ideal mechanism here, but it does have a major inconvenience: when the element just entered must be placed close to the beginning of the array, all the remaining elements must be moved one place to the right (or to the bottom, depending on how you visualize an array) to make room for the new one. If the incoming elements are nearly in ascending order, or if the number of elements is not too big, the delay can be tolerated. When the array is big, however, the process becomes too slow and impractical.

In program INSERT, line 10 asks for the number of elements to sort. Line 20 starts the FOR loop that will look for the position of the new element (T%) in the array. If the loop is terminated in line 30, the new element is greater than all the others in M% and therefore must be placed in the last position, M%(I%). If a number greater than T% is found, line 40 moves every element in the array from the position found (J%) to I%, and T% is placed in M%(J%), preserving the order.

A big advantage of this sort over the others presented is that after the insertion or deletion of an element, the order is preserved. An insertion sort is faster then a shuttle sort and slower than a shell sort, but if an element is added to a sorted array, both the shuttle and shell sorts must start the process from the beginning. The shell sort is fast when the array is in order, but still much too slow compared with the insertion sort in this particular situation.

```
0 '
                       ** INSERT **
                      Insertion sort

10 HOME: INPUT"NUMBER OF ITEMS TO SORT: ";N%:
   DIM M%(N%):
   FOR I%=1 TO N%: T%=INT(1000*RND)
20    FOR J%=1 TO I%:
         IF T%<M%(J%)
            THEN
               40
30    NEXT: M%(I%)=T%: GOTO 70
40    FOR K%=I% TO J% STEP-1:
         M%(K%)=M%(K%-1):
      NEXT
50    M%(J%)=T%
70    PRINT CHR$(13); I%; :
   NEXT I%
80 FOR I%=1 TO N%:
      PRINT M%(I%); :
   NEXT
```

Program 3.7

3.8 POINTERS

A completely different sorting technique can be used if the elements of the array are considered to be part of what is called a linked list. Though slower than a shell sort (but faster than a shuttle sort—by now you will have realized that virtually anything is faster than a shuttle sort), a sort using pointers is such that when one element is eliminated or inserted, the order is preserved, thus, with only a few interchanges.

Let's look at an example. Figure 3.7 shows a list with three numbers: 13, 29, and 40. Every element has a pointer to the next one.

Figure 3.7

Now, suppose we want to add the number 17 to the list. Figure 3.8 shows the method used. Notice that the rest of the list is not moved, and only the pointers are rearranged to keep it sorted. To list the array in order, all you have to do is follow the pointers.

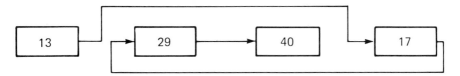

Figure 3.8

To translate this idea into BASIC, let's use a two dimensional array: the elements M%(x,0) will be the pointers, and the M%(x,1) will be the actual numbers. In the pointer, we will use the index of the next element. (If M%(x,0) = 3, for example the next element is in M%(3,1), and its pointer to the next is in M%(3,0).) To find the first element of the list, we must use a special element (usually called the head). We will use M%(0,0), and, since M%(0,1) is unused, we will use it to store the current number of elements in the list. Since the elements will be in positions 1 and greater, we can use zero to indicate the end of the list (EOL).

Now we want to insert the number 17. M%(0,1) tells us that there are three elements in the list; therefore, we can put the 17 in the first unoccupied position, M%(4,1). We must look for the position of this new number and rearrange the pointers accordingly. In this case, the 17 should go between the 13 and the 29. We move the pointer of the 13

(M%(1,0) = 2—therefore, the next element is in position M%(2,1)) to the pointer of the 17 (so that it points to the next element of the list, the 29) and set the pointer of the 13 to 4, the position of the 17. Figure 3.9 shows the new arrangement. Notice that besides the 17, which was copied, only two more numbers had to change, and this is true for lists of any size. However, finding the place of the new number is not as fast as in a binary search. More on that later.

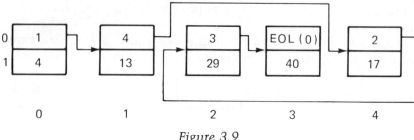

Figure 3.9

The process of printing the list in order is as follows. We look at the head, M%(0,0). If it is 0, we know that the list is empty, and we need not bother with it. Otherwise, we use the number in the head as the index of the next element. We print the value of this number and get its pointer, which in turn we use as the index for the next element. The process is repeated until we find that the index in an element is zero, our convention for the end of the list (EOL). Searching for an element is similar, the only difference being that we can stop when we find it.

Deleting an element from the list is slightly more complicated. Starting with the situation of Figure 3.9, suppose we wish to eliminate the 29. First, we look for it. Besides searching, we must store the previous pointer, or else we cannot redirect the list as we did when we added the 17. In Figure 3.10 we see the first step of the deletion. TEMP is used to remember the position of the 29 because now it has been deleted from the list.

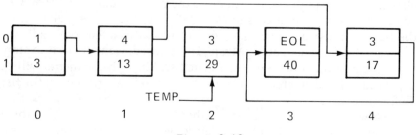

Figure 3.10

If we listed the sorted file at this point, we would see that the order is correct and that 29 has actually been deleted. However, there is an empty spot in the array, and if we leave it there, there will be no way to get it back, and as more elements are deleted, the array will be able to store fewer and fewer numbers.

Figure 3.11 shows that second step of the deletion, in which we move the last element of the list to the position previously occupied by 29. Notice that, since we want to move the last element, we must know which element is pointing to it. (We had to know that M%(1,0) was pointing to the 17.)

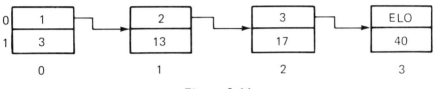

Figure 3.11

If the list is very long, looking for an element can take a long time and make the process impractical. A binary search cannot be used because the list is sorted sequentially, and we do not know which is the middle element of the list until we read all the previous ones. I have devised what I call a pseudo-binary search, which, if not as efficient as the one described in Section 3.3, is nonetheless much faster on the average than the sequential search. The method is as follows: Suppose we want to find a number E. We look for the size of the list in (M%(0,1)) and use the integer part of the square root of that number as a GUIDE.[2] We scan the array every GUIDE positions, looking for a number which is smaller than, but not equal to, E. We achieve nothing if we find the position of E in the array: we need the *element* that is *pointing* to E. At the end of the scan, we will have found a number which is smaller than E but, hopefully, close to it, and we can proceed with the usual linked search. In the worst case we will make roughly the same number of comparisons as in an ordinary sequential search, but when E is not close to the beginning of the list, the search will be much shorter.

In the pseudo-binary search of program LINKED, we start with the value $-1.70141E+38$ (this is minus machine infinity, or the smallest number representable by the language) as the initial

---

[2]If $Q = Sqr(N)$, the array is divided into Q parts of equal length (except perhaps the last), each one with Q elements.

minimum to which every number obtained with GUIDE is compared. If the number is smaller than E, it replaces the minimum. At the end of the subroutine DELETE, since we no longer have the pointer to the last element of the list, we use a sequential search to look for it. Use of a pseudo-binary search to find it improves the average performance and is left as an exercise.

```
0  '
                        ** LINKED **
                Linked list using pointers.

5  HOME
10 DEFINT A-L,N-Z:DIM M(1000,1):MIN=-1.70141E+38
20 NIL=0:M(0,0)=NIL:M(0,1)=0:FALSE=0:TRUE=-1:FL=-1
30 PRINT"1-Add":
   PRINT"2-Find":
   PRINT"3-Delete":
   PRINT"4-List ";
40 W$=INPUT$(1):V=VAL(W$):
   IF V<1 OR V>4
          THEN
              40
50 ON V GOTO 100,200,300,400
100 PRINT:INPUT"Number to add : ";E:GOSUB 5000
110 GOTO 30
200 PRINT:INPUT"Number to find:";E
210 GOSUB 7000:
    IF J=0
      THEN
          PRINT"Not found ":GOTO 230
220 PRINT E" Is in position "J
230 GOSUB 10000:GOTO 30
300 PRINT:INPUT"Number to delete : ";E
310 GOSUB 9000:
    IF J=0
      THEN
          PRINT"Not found ":GOTO 330
320 PRINT "Deleted"
330 GOSUB 10000:GOTO 30
400 GOSUB 6000:GOSUB 10000:GOTO 30
5000 '
                        ** Add **

5010 N=M(0,1):M(N+1,1)=E
5020 J=0
5030 GOSUB 8000
5040 IF M(J,0)=NIL
        THEN
            M(J,0)=N+1:M(N+1,0)=NIL:M(0,1)=N+1:K=J:
            RETURN
5050 L=J:J=M(J,0)
5060 V=M(J,1):
     IF E>V
        THEN
```

```
         5040
5070 M(L,0)=N+1·M(N+1,0)-J:M(0,1)-N+1:K=L:RETURN
6000 JJ=0:PRINT
6010 JJ=M(JJ,0):
     IF JJ=NIL
        THEN
          PRINT:RETURN
6020 PRINT M(JJ,1);:GOTO 6010
7000 '
                    ** Search **

7020 J=0:
     IF M(J,0)=NIL
        THEN
          RETURN
7030 L=J:J=M(J,0)
7040 IF M(J,1)=E
        THEN
          RETURN
7050 IF M(J,1)>E OR M(J,0)=NIL
        THEN
           J=0:RETURN
7070 GOTO 7030
8000 '
             ** Pseudo-binary search **

8010 IF M(0,1)=0
        THEN
          J=0:RETURN
8020 P=M(0,0):M.SMALL=MIN:FL=FALSE
8030 FOR I=1 TO M(0,1) STEP 20
8040    J=M(I,0):
        TEMP=M(J,1):
        IF TEMP>E
          THEN
             8070
8050    IF TEMP=E
          THEN
            RETURN
8060    IF TEMP>M.SMALL
          THEN
             P=J:M.SMALL=TEMP:FL=TRUE
8070 NEXT:
     IF FL
        THEN
          J=P:RETURN
8080 J=0:RETURN
9000 '
                    ** Delete **

9010 GOSUB 7000:
     IF J=0
        THEN
          RETURN
9020 N=M(0,1):
```

```
      IF  M(J,0)=N
         THEN
            M(L,0)=J:GOTO 9025
9022  M(L,0)=M(J,0)
9025  IF  J=N
         THEN
            9040
9030  M(J,0)=M(N,0):M(J,1)=M(N,1):
      IF  K<>J
         THEN
            M(K,0)=J
9040  N=N-1:M(0,1)=N:
      FOR I=0 TO N-1:
         IF  M(I,0)=N
         THEN
            K=I:RETURN
9050  NEXT:RETURN
10000 PRINT"Press any key ";:W$=INKEY$
10010 W$=INPUT$(1):PRINT:RETURN
```

Program 3.8

3.9 MERGE SORT

When you have two arrays that are already sorted, and you want to combine them into a third one, there is a very simple way to do it. First, compare the first two elements of the arrays, and send the smaller to the third array. Then, compare the two first elements that have not been sent to the third array, and again send the smaller one. Repeat the process until one of the two arrays runs out of numbers (or strings), and then copy the remaining numbers directly into the third array. Let's look at an example. Figure 3.12 shows the two sorted arrays that are to be merged. In the first step, 5 is compared with 1, and, since 1 is smaller, it is copied into the third array. (The arrow shows that the 1 was placed in the first position of the third array.) Then 5 and 6 are compared, and 5 is copied. The process is repeated until the second array runs out of numbers (after the 14 is copied). At that point, the rest of the first array (20 and 24) is copied directly, without comparisons.

When a file must be sorted and is too big to fit in memory, none of the methods so far described affords an easy way of sorting the file. (The tagfile method can help sort in disk, but it is limited, too.) What we can do, however, is read as much of the file as can fit in memory, sort it with any method (the faster, the better), write it back into a file with a name different from the original one, and repeat the process until the entire file has been broken into small sorted files. Then, since a

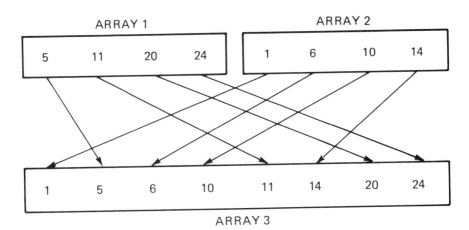

Figure 3.12

merge sort needs to compare only two numbers, two of these small files can be merged into a third one, which in turn can be merged with another small one, and so forth, until the entire file is reconstructed, this time entirely sorted.

Program MERGE expects the number of elements in the file as the first element. The sum of the numbers read from the two files is printed as the first element of the new file. The files are then read, one element at a time, and the numbers sent to the third file in ascending order.

```
0  '
                    ** MERGE **
              Merge two sorted files in disk

10  INPUT"FILES TO MERGE ";N1$,N2$:INPUT"INTO ";N3$:
    OPEN"I",1,N1$:OPEN"I",2,N2$:OPEN"O",3,N3$
20  INPUT#1,N1:INPUT#2,N2:I1=1:I2=1:
    INPUT#1,M1:INPUT#2,M2:PRINT#3,N1+N2
30  WHILE I1<=N1 AND I2<=N2
40    IF M1>M2
        THEN
          PRINT #3,M2:I2=I2+1:
          IF I2>N2
            THEN
              100
            ELSE
              INPUT#2,M2:GOTO 100
        ELSE
50        PRINT #3,M1:I1=I1+1:
          IF I1>N1
```

```
            THEN
                100
            ELSE
                INPUT#1,M1
100 WEND
110 IF I2>N2
        THEN
            PRINT #3,M1:
            FOR I1=I1+1 TO N1:
               INPUT#1,M1:PRINT #3,M1:
            NEXT
        ELSE
            PRINT #3,M2:
            FOR I2=I2+1 TO N2:
               INPUT#2,M2:PRINT #3,M2:
            NEXT
120 PRINT:CLOSE
```

Program 3.9

3.10 QUICKSORT

We include here a sorting method that, on the average, is faster than all the others so far discussed. Since understanding it is more complicated than understanding the other methods, only the program is given.[3]

```
O '
                    ** QCKSORT **
                      Quicksort

 10 INPUT"Number of items ";N%:
    DIM ND%(N%),L%(N%),R%(N%)
 20 FOR I%=1 TO N%:
       ND%(I%)=INT(1000*RND):
    NEXT
 30 GOSUB 7460
 40 FOR I%=1 TO N%:
       PRINT ND%(I%);:
    NEXT:
    END

7460 '
                  ** QUICKSORT **

7480 S1%=1:L%(1)=1:R%(1)=N%
7560 WHILE S1%>0:
       L1%=L%(S1%):R1%=R%(S1%):S1%=S1%-1:
```

---

[3]For an explanation of Quicksort, see *Fundamentals of Data Structures* by Ellis Horowitz and Sartaj Sahni (Computer Science Press, Rockville, Maryland, 1978).

```
        L2%=L1%:R2%=R1%
7620    L2%=L1%:R2%=R1%
7660    X%=ND%((L1%+R1%)\2)
7700    WHILE ND%(L2%)<X%:
            L2%=L2%+1:
        WEND
7780    WHILE X%<ND%(R2%):
            R2%=R2%-1:
        WEND
7880    IF L2%<=R2%
            THEN
                T%=ND%(L2%):ND%(L2%)=ND%(R2%):
                ND%(R2%)=T%:L2%=L2%+1:R2%=R2%-1
7980    IF L2%<=R2%
            THEN
                7700
8020    IF L2%<R1%
            THEN
                S1%=S1%+1:L%(S1%)=L2%:
                R%(S1%)=R1%:R1%=R2%:
                IF L1%<R1%
                    THEN
                        7620
8080    R1%=R2%:
        IF L1%<R1%
            THEN
                7620
8120    PRINT CHR$(13);S1%;:
        WEND
8140 PRINT:RETURN
```

Program 3.10

3.11 COMPARISON

Table 3.1 shows the sorting times for the programs presented in this section.

SORT	NO. OF ITEMS							
	50	100	250	500	750	1000	2500	5000
SHUTTLE	12	47	4:44	16:51	36:17	1:10:48	7:06:34	27:39:39
INSERTION	10	34	3:17	12:39	28:12	50:10	–	–
INSERTION (b. search)	13	37	2:43	8:43	18:31	31:44	–	–

SHELL	8	20	1:00	2:18	3:51	5:27	16:05	36:51
LINKED	23	49	2:53	7:04	12:03	18:06	1:17:08	–
QUICKSORT	8	16	48	1:42	2:39	3:40	10:32	‡

‡ Five thousand did not fit in memory with Quicksort. It took 16:40 to sort 4000.

Table 3.1

Exercises

1. Write a program to sort a disk file using a tagfile. Every entry should have more than one element (name and address, for example). Read only the key, and store the tagfile as a separate sequential file.

2. Modify the insertion sort of Section 3.7 so that an element can be not only inserted but also deleted.

3. Write a program combining the speed of either the shell sort or the quicksort with the convenience of addition and deletion of single elements as per the insertion sort.

4. Write a program to sort a disk file using a disk tagfile, with the pointers of the tagfile being the first of every record in the disk. Only two numbers of the tagfile must be in memory at any one time.

5. Modify program LINKED so that the pointer to the last element is found by means of a pseudobinary search.

6. Modify program INSERTION so that the search for the position of the new number is done by a binary search. To see the improvement in performance, see Table 3.1.

7. Think of an algorithm to sort with only one FOR loop (and only one loop altogether). If you only compare and interchange contiguous elements of the array, the need for the second loop is eliminated. This is probably the simplest kind of sort, but its performance is much worse than the shuttle sort!

8. Split keys are a very useful concept. Suppose you have to sort books in a library by author, and books of the same author by title. You could use one sort for the names and a second one for the titles, but it is not as easy as it sounds at first. A much easier way is to do only one sort, using as key both author and title. For example, if you had the arrays AUTHOR$ and TITLE$, the comparisons could be

IF AUTHOR$(I) + TITLE$(I) > AUTHOR$(J) + TITLE$(J) THEN . .,

Or you could create a parallel array (if you have enough memory) with every AUTHOR$ and TITLE$ together. Write a program to sort a library by author, title, and edition.

9. Write a program to sort a sequential file in which the entries are strings of different lengths. Use intermediate random access files and the merge sort, and leave the final file in sequential form.

DISK FILES

4

BASIC-80 can only address up to 64 K bytes, so even if your computer has a bigger memory, you will not be able to access it directly. Disks usually provide a storage capacity much larger than 64 K bytes, though accessing them is slower than accessing the main memory. Besides offering this greater storage, disks are a very convenient and economical way of keeping programs and data that must be preserved when the computer is turned off.[1]

In this book, we consider a file as a (possibly empty) collection of characters or numbers which reside on a disk, and a field as one of the items written in the file (a single string or a single value). We are not concerned with whether the disk is a 5-½ inch or an 8 inch floppy disk, a hard disk, or any equivalent device,[2] because we are not going to deal with the actual process of writing to the disk. We leave that to the operating system and to BASIC.

---

[1]There are two types of nonvolatile memories:

The ferrite core, which is now obsolete and not used in any microcomputer.

The bubble memory, which is slower than the dynamic and static types found in most microcomputers. The price of bubble memory has been dropping slowly but is still too high to allow it to replace the types used today. Bubble memory sometimes replaces a disk drive in portable computers.

[2]Now there are 3-inch diskettes on the market, removable 5-½-inch hard disks, tape cartridges that can read both sequentially and in random access mode, and even batteries of diskettes that behave like a hard disk.

Each of the two types of files—sequential and random access—supported by BASIC has its own advantages and disadvantages. It is up to you to decide which method suits your application best. There are, however, a few points and techniques that you should know in order to have your files make optimal use of the capabilities of the disk.

The default number of files that can be processed simultaneously by BASIC-80 is 3. However, you can change this number and process from zero to 15 simultaneously. Read the initialization of BASIC-80 in the corresponding manual. Another default value is 128 bytes for the disk buffers, and it also can be changed at the initialization level.

4.1 SEQUENTIAL FILES

In this type of file, the information is written to the disk in sequence; that is, the different items are written one by one, so that to write the third item, for example, we must first write the second one. The chief advantages of sequential files are:

1. Economy of space; the files contain exactly the strings or numbers written to it, a separator, and nothing else.

2. Easy manipulation; the creation and retrieval of a sequential file is easy: there are no calculations to make, and a single command is enough to start writing to the file or reading from it.

Chief disadvantages of sequential files are:

1. To read a field, all the previous ones must be read also.

2. To change even one item, the entire file must be reread and rewritten.

INPUT# and LINE INPUT# behave exactly as their counterparts in input from the keyboard. (See section 1.1.) If you want to read every field exactly as it was printed to the files, including spaces, commas, and colons, use LINE INPUT#. If you must stick in INPUT#, use WRITE# instead of PRINT#: WRITE# surrounds every string and number with quotes.

The BASIC-80 manual has several examples of sequential files—how to create a sequential file, how to read it, and how to update it.

4.1.1 BUFFERING

When you issue an INPUT# or PRINT#, your data is not necessarily written to the disk immediately. Special areas of memory called *disk buffers* are used as temporary storage before the actual transfers between memory and disk take place. Figure 4.1 shows the contents of a small buffer (remember that the default size is 128 bytes— in the example the buffer has only 30 bytes) after the execution of each instruction.

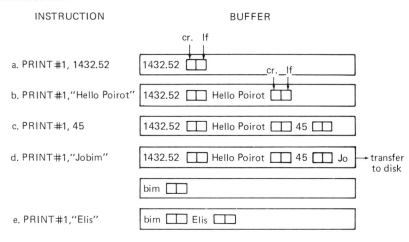

Figure 4.1

As is plain from Figure 4.1d, only when the buffer is full is there an actual transfer to disk, and sometimes a field ends up split into two different buffers. When the file is being read, the process is exactly the same in reverse order: the buffer is brought into memory, and the fields are taken one by one until a new buffer must be transferred from disk, as shown in Figure 4.2.

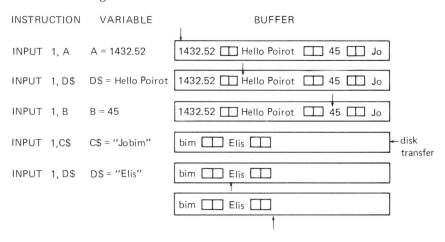

Figure 4.2

When a program is going to execute most of its work on random access files, it is a good idea to have big buffers, so that the actual transfers between memory and disk (which occur at a slower rate than does access to the information in the buffer) are minimized. Suppose you have two large files which are going to be merged into a third one with the merge sort described in Section 3.9. With regular-sized buffers, the frequent disk accesses will delay the process. If, on the other hand, you have instructed BASIC to reserve big buffers at the moment of initialization, every disk access will bring to memory enough information to work for some time. Likewise, the resulting file will be temporarily written to the buffer and transferred to the disk much less frequently. Example 4.1 shows the initialization command for buffers of 2000 bytes each. (Your version of BASIC might be called differently, but everything else is the same.)

```
MBASIC /S:2000
```

Example 4.1 Buffer initialization

4.1.2 LOW-LEVEL ACCESS

Certain control characters or sequences of control characters have special meanings in the different operating systems, and their use can lead to unexpected results. Let's look at an example.
The sequence carriage return-line feed (CHR$(13),CHR$(10)) is used to separate fields. Example 4.2 shows a sequence of lines that results in misreading a file because of the presence of this sequence in the file.

```
10 W$="Hello "+CHR$(13)+CHR$(10)+" there, ":A$=" Pete"
20 OPEN"O",1,"FILE":PRINT#1,W$:PRINT#1,A$:CLOSE
30 OPEN"I",1,"FILE":INPUT#1,W$:INPUT#1,A$
```

Example 4.2 Erroneous string retrieval

After line 30 is executed, W$ = "Hello" and A$ = " there, ". Since "Pete" has not been read yet, all the subsequent fields will be 'out of phase' and might end up being read into the wrong variables.

To allow use of these special characters in a sequential file, you must retrieve one character at a time, analyze it, and process it before returning its contents. The command INPUT$(1,#X) reads one character from the file. (X is the number of the file; 1 indicates that only one character should be read, but any number from 1 to 255 can be used.)

4.2 RANDOM ACCESS FILES

The biggest advantage of the random access file is that its fields can be accessed directly without touching the rest of the file. Any field can be deleted or changed, and new ones can be added, regardless of the size of the file. The chief disadvantage is that it can waste a lot of disk space. In order to have immediate access to any field, the file is divided into records of equal size. To achieve this homogeneity, spaces must be used when strings are smaller than the maximum size reserved, and numerical values must be stored with a fixed size.

In this section we shall look at some details of the process of creation and retrieval of random access files, as well as some useful extra features not available in the sequential type of file. The BASIC manual has some useful examples, too.

After the file is OPENed in random access mode (specified by the "R" in the file mode part of the OPEN command), the buffer assigned to the file must be formatted or fielded to gain access to it. Figure 4.3 shows the contents of the buffer after execution of the command

FIELD#1,4 AS CODE$,25 AS NAME$,2 AS AGE$

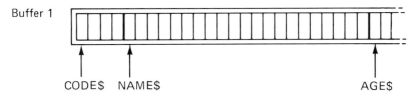

Figure 4.3

The three variables CODE$, NAME$, and AGE$ are now pointing to the buffer and cannot be used in the left-hand side of a LET (assignment) statement. Notice that we are going to use 31 bytes of the buffer, and it has room (in the default case) for 128. More than one FIELD can be executed on the same buffer, and the string variables used can be simultaneously active.

LSET AND RSET

Let's suppose that you have your data ready and want to write it to the disk. The first step is to transfer it to the buffer by means of

LSET or RSET, which copy a string from one string variable into another (in this case a buffer variable). If the source string is too long to fit in the destination, the extra characters are chopped off (always from the right of the string). If the source string is shorter than the destination allows, spaces are added to the right (LSET) or left (RSET) of the string to fill the destination, so that the previous contents of the source are completely erased. LSET and RSET always preserve the length of the destination variable.[3]

MKI$, MKS$, MKD$; CVI, CVS, CVD

Since only strings can be sent to the buffer, a conversion must be made before the transfer of numbers via LSET and RSET. If STR$ is used, the resulting string will have an unpredictable length. Every type of variable has a set number of bytes associated with it: integer variables take two bytes, single-precision variables take four, and double-precision variables take eight. The representation scheme used is beyond the scope of this book, but except for some cases of integer values, the contents of these bytes cannot be directly converted to their numerical equivalents.

The three functions MKI$, MKS$, and MKD$ take the contents of a numeric variable (or a numeric expression) and return a string which is a copy of the internal representation. For example, if $E = 142.857$, STR$(E) will return the string " 142.857", of length eight. (A space is added to the left to leave room for the sign.) MKS$(E) will return a string of length four because single-precision variables always take four bytes, regardless of their contents. An attempt to print this string will result in a strange and meaningless (for the human reader, not the computer) sequence of characters. Likewise, converting it to numerical form with VAL will produce a number which has no relation to the original E.

MKI$ must be used with integer variables, MKS$ with single-precision variables, and MKD$ with double precision. To convert the strings produced by these functions back into their numerical forms, there is another set of functions: CVI, CVS, and CVD (which correspond, of course, to integer, single-precision and double-precision variables). They take a string as argument and return the equivalent number. If the length of the string does not correspond with the ex-

---

[3]Since LSET and RSET do not affect the resulting length of strings, no relocation takes place, except when the destination string is in program memory.

pected type, an 'illegal function call' makes the program halt.

The procedure to move a numerical value to the file is, then, to convert the number to a string with one of the MKx$ functions, use LSET or RSET to move it to the buffer, and execute a PUT. To retrieve it, simply GET the buffer and use one of the CVx functions to convert it back to its numerical form.

The use of these functions guarantees a homogeneous length and economizes space when the numbers have many significant digits. For example, the number $-1.357924680765432 + D34$ would require 22 characters in string form, but it can be saved with only eight. The integer 28564 would be six characters long, but is only two when treated with the MKI$ function.

Study the following example:

NUMBER = 97865

PERSON$ = "Frau Bruhard"

YEARS = 55

Program 4.1 transfers the contents of the variables (what is to the right of the equals signs) to the buffer and PUTs them on the disk. Figure 4.4 shows the process.

```
10 OPEN"R",1,"DEMOFILE"
20 FIELD#1,4 AS CODE$,25 AS NAME.$,2 AS AGE$
30 NUMBER=97865:PERSON$="Frau Bruhard":YEARS=55
40 LSET CODE$=MKS$(NUMBER)
50 LSET NAME.$=PERSON$
60 LSET AGE$=MKI$(YEARS)
70 PUT 1,1
80 CLOSE
```

Program 4.1

4.2.1 THE RECORD LENGTH PARAMETER

When you OPEN a file in random access mode, every PUT and GET moves the default buffer of 128 bytes. If your record length is much shorter than the buffer size, every time you write a record, you use one block the size of a buffer, as shown in Figure 4.5.

You can economize space by specifying the length of your record when you OPEN the file by adding a comma and the record length to the OPEN command. For example, after executing the command

10 OPEN"R",1,"FILE",15

the buffer will be 'partitioned' into smaller pieces of 15 bytes, as shown in Figure 4.6.

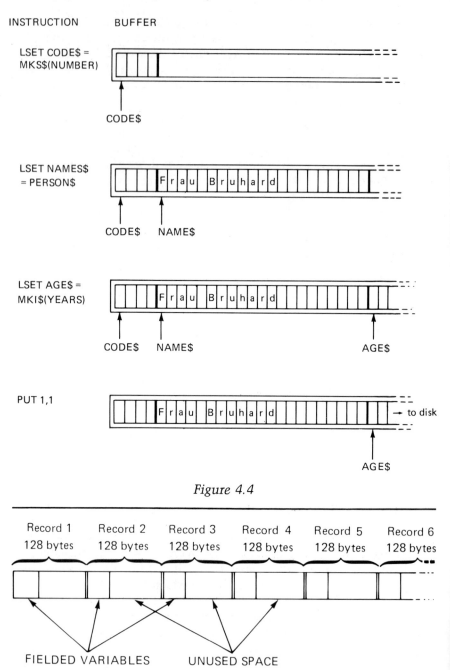

Figure 4.4

Figure 4.5

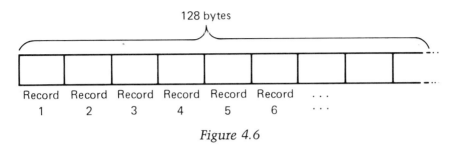

Figure 4.6

4.2.2 VIRTUAL MEMORY FOR ARRAYS

When handling very large arrays, it is easy to run out of memory. The result is that there is no way to run the program. If you can tolerate the slower speed, an alternative is to have the array on disk. However, since random access files are indexed sequentially,[4] only one-dimensional arrays correspond directly to the indexing scheme of file records. Thus, some discussion on the storage method for multi-dimensional arrays is worthwhile.

A one-dimensional array can be visualized as a collection of objects (integers, strings, etc.) that are stored sequentially, with element number two immediately after number one and before number three, as shown in Figure 4.7. We will suppose that all arrays start with index 1, as if OPTION BASE 1 had been executed: no element with index zero will be allowed.

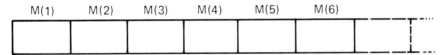

Figure 4.7

With two dimensions, the representation cannot be sequential, and we must make a decision about the order of the different elements. A possible scheme is shown in Figure 4.8, where an array DIMensioned as (3,4) is taken apart by rows and reassembled in sequential form. If we want to access the element with indices (2,3) (2 is the index of the column, 3 that of row—therefore, element (2,3) contains 0.5), we have to traverse two rows (six elements, because N = 3), and then two more elements, for a total of eight.

---

[4]You can access record 45, for M(45), but an element of a two-dimensional array, for example M(12,23), does not have an immediate counterpart in the file.

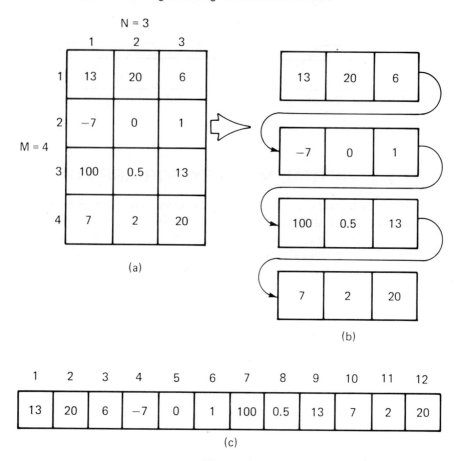

Figure 4.8

To calculate the elements in the rows traversed, we take the row index (3 in the example), subtract 1 from it (since we do not have to traverse the row where the element is, only the previous ones), and multiply the result by the number of elements in each row (N in this example). This leaves us in the desired row, so we add the column index. The resulting number is the position in the sequential representation (8 in the example). If we agree that N will store the number of elements per row and M the number of elements per column, with (I,J) representing the element in column I, row J, the formula to get the sequential position is

POSITION = (J − 1) * N + I

which can easily be written as a function, as shown in Function 4.1.

```
10 DEF FN POSITION(I,J)=(J-1)*N+I.
```

Function 4.1 Sequential position

Note that N is used as a global variable, whereas I and J are local and can be replaced by the indices. If more than one array of this type is to be processed in the same program, the N DIMension could be sent as a parameter, too.

Three-dimensional arrays follow the same pattern, but are slightly harder to visualize. Suppose an array is DIMensioned M(4,2,3). Use N = 4, M = 2, and O = 3 to denote the size of each dimension, and (I,J,K) as indices in the three dimensions. Figure 4.9 shows one representation of this arrangement. We first transform the three-dimensional array into a two-dimensional array, which we know how to handle.

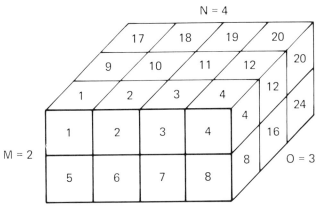

Figure 4.9

In Figure 4.10 the blocks have been cut and are on their way to becoming one long block of only two dimensions. The latter is shown in Figure 4.11.

If the process of Figure 4.8 is now applied to this block, the result is the sequential representation partially shown in Figure 4.12.

Now let's look for an element, say M(4,2,2). In Figure 4.9 this element is labeled '16'. To get to it, we must first traverse a whole block of N*M, that is, 8, elements. Then we must leave behind a block of N elements, that is, 4 more. Finally, we must move four more positions (as specified by the I index) to get to M(4,2,2). The process can be summarized as

POSITION = (K − 1) * M * N + (J − 1) * N + I

The function form is shown in Function 4.2.

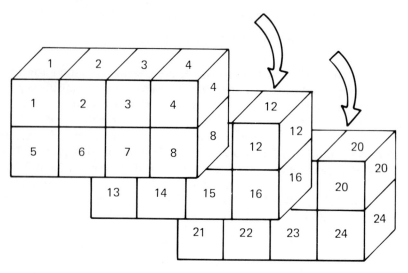

Figure 4.10

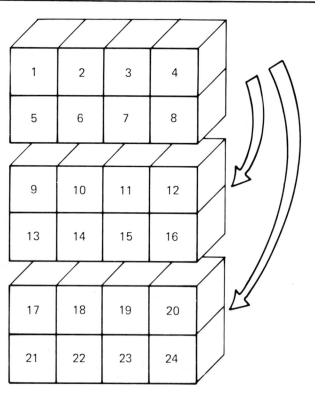

Figure 4.11

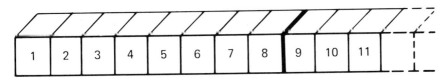

Figure 4.12

```
10 DEF FN POSITION(I,J,K)=(K-1)*N*M+(J-1)*N+I
```

Function 4.2 Sequential three-dimensional array

Comparing Functions 4.1 and 4.2, you will see a pattern that will let you write the functions for arrays with more than three dimensions.

We now have the information necessary to store arrays in disk. Let's suppose that the elements of our array are single-precision numbers and that the DIMensions we want are (20,30,40). The total number of elements is 20*30*40 = 24,000 (remember that the indices begin with 1, not 0), which will not fit in memory: every single-precision variable requires four bytes, and our array would need 96,000, more than the 64 K that BASIC can access. Program 4.2 stores and recalls elements of the array as if they were stored directly in memory. Since it uses the indices to access every element, this program can easily be modified to suit your particular needs. The limit on the size of the array (or arrays) is the size of your disk.

```
              ** VIRTUAL **
         Virtual array in disk file

10 DEF FN POSITION(I,J,K)=(K-1)*N*M+(J-1)*N+I
20 HOME
30 INPUT"N,M,O : ";N,M,O
40 OPEN"R",1,"DUMMY",4:FIELD 1,4 AS A$
60 INPUT"I,J,K ";I,J,K
70 PRINT"1-STORE, 2-RECALL ";
80 W$=INPUT$(1):
   IF W$="1"
      THEN
         90
      ELSE
         IF W$="2"
            THEN
               110
            ELSE
               80
90 PRINT:INPUT"VALUE ";VALUE:LSET A$=MKS$(VALUE)
100 PUT 1,FN POSITION(I,J,K):GOTO 60
110 GET 1,FN POSITION(I,J,K):V=CVS(A$):PRINT V:
    GOTO 60
```

Program 4.2

Initialization

When you use a numeric array for the first time, BASIC sets all its elements to 0. When you OPEN a random file, no initialization takes place, so it is your responsibility to initialize it.

4.2.3 MORE THAN 32,767 RECORDS

The maximum record number allowed is 32,767, more than sufficient for most purposes. However, there are circumstances that require a larger number. Consider the case in which you want to use the disk to store an array M(40,40,40), of which every element is an integer. Since the largest element will be 40*40*40 = 64,000, neither a GET nor a PUT can be used. An easy way to resolve this difficulty is to have two (or more) files opened simultaneously, one of which is used for the first 32,767 elements, and the second one for those from 32,768 on. In other words, when the number returned by FN POSITION is greater than 32,767, the number will be PUT in the second file (which must have a different name, possibly different only in the last character). Program 4.3 keeps the two files OPEN and subtracts 32,767 from the value returned by FN POSITION when it is too big to fit in the first file; so, the record that would have been 32,768 actually becomes number 1 of the second file.

```
0  '    ** More than 32767 records **
10 HOME
20 OPEN"R",1,"ARRAY1",2:OPEN"R",2,"ARRAY2",2
30 FIELD 1,2 AS A$:FIELD 2,2 AS B$
40 DEF FN POSITION(I,J,K)=(K-1)*N*M+(J-1)*N+I
50 PRINT"1-Write":PRINT"2-Read":PRINT"3-Quit ";
60 W$=INPUT$(1):
   IF W$<"1"OR W$>"3"
     THEN
        60
     ELSE
        ON VAL(W$) GOTO 70,150,200
70 INPUT"Value ";VALUE%
80 GOSUB 500
100 ON FILE GOTO 110,120
110 LSET A$=MKI$(VALUE%):PUT 1,REC:GOTO 50
120 LSET B$=MKI$(VALUE%):PUT 2,REC:GOTO 50
150 GOSUB 500
160 ON FILE GOTO 170,180
170 GET 1,REC:VALUE%=CVI(A$):PRINT VALUE%:GOTO 50
180 GET 2,REC:VALUE%=CVI(B$):PRINT VALUE%:GOTO 50
200 CLOSE:END
500 INPUT"Position (i,j,k) ";I,J,K:
    REC=FN POSITION(I,J,K)
510 IF REC>32767
```

```
        THEN
           RCC=RCC 32767:FILE=2
        ELSE
           FILE=1
  520 RETURN
```

Program 4.3

4.2.4 STORING CONTROL CHARACTERS

In Section 4.1.1 we saw that creating a sequential file with control characters in it can cause problems. Random access files are immune to this problem, since they do not use INPUT# or LINE INPUT#, and LSET and RSET copy strings directly into the buffer without changing them in any way. To store sequential data in a random access file, a special buffering technique can be used. Program 4.4 reads one character in line 30, echoes it on the screen, adds it to X$ (the equivalent of BUFF$ of the input subroutines), and checks the resulting length. If X$ has exactly 128 characters, it is copied into the buffer by LSET, then N (the current number of records) is incremented, and the buffer is sent to the disk by executing a PUT. The new value of N is also PUT in the disk (in record number one), and the program continues.

When the file is read, line 70 GETs the value of N and then reads and prints N strings of 128 characters each. Notice that we are not storing X$ before it has 128 characters. Some decision must be made as to what to do with it before the file is CLOSEd.

```
                       ** FASTFILE **
           Fast screen with random access storage.

  20 OPEN"R",1,"DUMMY",128:FIELD 1,128 AS A$:
     FIELD 1,4 AS B$:CTRL.X$=CHR$(24):N=1:
     HOME:WIDTH(255)
  25 PRINT"1-DRAW":PRINT"2-READ ";
  26 W$=INPUT$(1):
     IF W$="1"
        THEN
           HOME:GOTO 30
        ELSE
           IF W$="2"
              THEN
                 70
              ELSE
                 26
  30 W$=INPUT$(1):
     IF W$=CTRL.X$
        THEN
           50
  40 X$=X$+W$:PRINT W$;:
```

```
    IF LEN(X$)=128
       THEN
          N=N+1:LSET A$=X$:PUT 1,N:
          LSET B$=MKS$(N):PUT 1,1:X$="":GOTO 30
       ELSE
          30
50 HOME:
   FOR I=2 TO N:
      GET 1,I:PRINT A$;:
   NEXT:
   IF X$<>""
      THEN
         PRINT X$;
60 GOTO 30
70 GET 1,1:N=CVS(B$)
80 HOME:
   FOR I=2 TO N:
      GET 1,I:PRINT A$;:
   NEXT:
   IF X$<>""
      THEN
         PRINT X$;
90 GOTO 90
```

Program 4.4

Exercises

1. A random access file is to be used to store an array. Write a program in sequential mode that opens the file and initializes all the elements of the virtual array to zero.

2. Write a function to find the sequential position of an array DIMensioned as M(2,4,3,5,1).

3. Write a function to find the sequential position of a three-dimensional array using the subscripts zero, as in the default case.

4. The method used in Section 4.2.4 lets you write sequential files using the advantages of the random access mode. Using the first two bytes to store the size of the file, you can then append new entries without reading and writing the entire file. Write a program to create a sequential file and to append elements to it using this method.

USER-DEFINED FUNCTIONS

5

User-defined functions can be a very powerful tool in programming. Although they are not essential and can be replaced by subroutines or program fragments accessed by GOTO's, functions can make your programs clearer and your programming a lot easier. Once you have written a function and are sure of its correctness, you can forget about the way it performs its task and use it as if it were part of the language.

Suppose the function ABS(X) did not exist in BASIC and you needed it. Compare Program Fragments 5.1a and 5.1b.

```
a - 10 PRINT ABS(X),ABS(Y)

b - 10 TEMP=X:GOSUB 1000:PRINT TEMP,:TEMP=Y:GOSUB 1000:PRINT TEMP
     1000 IF TEMP<0
               THEN
                   TEMP=-TEMP
     1010 RETURN
```

Program Fragment 5.1

There is no doubt that 5.1b is much harder to write and understand, and as the complexity of your program grows, so does the possibility of losing track of variable names and jumps from one place to another. Likewise, when you have to read someone else's programs, or even one that you wrote but do not remember well, it will be much easier for you to understand if you defined your own functions and documented them well. BASIC-80 provides a whole variety of functions, but no language can provide a function for every need. It would have to be infinite to do that! However, BASIC-80 gives you the possibility of defining your own functions by means of the DEF FN statement:

DEF FN ⟨name⟩ (parameter list) = function definition

Name can be any valid variable name. The parameter list can have from one to 12 variables of any type. The function definition can be as long as a program line will allow. (If the function definition is very long, it is a good idea to use an entire line for that function alone).

Following are some of the conveniences and possibilities of user-defined functions.

Local or Global Variables

The variables used in the parameter list are local variables. Thus, they can be used in the function definition as many times as desired, and their use will not interfere with the values of the variables of the same name in the program. On the other hand, if a variable name that is used in the function definition does not appear in the parameter list, its current value in the program will be used in the evaluation. This way, local and global variables may be mixed in the function definition.

Deferred or Immediate Use

Once a function is defined by the DEF FN statement, it can be used anywhere, both in a program and at command level.

Multiple Parameters

Up to twelve variables of any type (string, integer, single precision, double precision) can be used in the parameter list. They can be used in any order, but when the function is invoked, the parameters passed must correspond to the types of the variable in the parameter list, or one of the following two types of errors can occur: 'type mismatch', when a string is sent where the function expects a number, or vice versa; and 'overflow', when the value sent is too big to fit in an integer variable.

String and Numerical Functions Supported

Not only numbers can be returned by user-defined functions: just as LEFT$ and MID$ return strings, you can make your own functions return a string by appending a dollar sign to the name of the function or by including the first letter of the function name in DEF STR statement.

All Numerical Types Supported

The function name accepts the three numerical type-definition symbols ("%", "!", and "#") as well as the type declarations DEFINT, DEFSNG, and DEFDBL. A function thus defined will return a value of the specified type.

Local Errors

When an error occurs in the evaluation of a function, the corresponding error message is printed, but the line number provided is the one where the function was invoked, not where the function was defined. Thus, invalid parameters or range errors are easier to spot.

5.1 STRING FUNCTIONS

Following are some useful string functions.

5.1.1 INSERT

Function INSERT (Function 5.1) inserts the string Y$ into X$, starting at position POSITION.

```
10 DEF FN INSERT$(X$,Y$,POSITION)=LEFT$(X$,POSITION-1)+
               Y$+RIGHT$(X$,LEN(X$)-POSITION+1)
```
Function 5.1 INSERT

Example:

PRINT FN INSERT("This house", "lovely ",6)

will print

This lovely house.

5.1.2 REMOVE

Function 5.2 removes a substring of length LENGTH from X$, starting at position START.

```
10 DEF FN REMOVE$(X$,START,LENGTH)=LEFT$(X$,START-1)+
               RIGHT$(X$,LEN(X$)-(START+LENGTH)+1)
```
Function 5.2 REMOVE

Example:

> PRINT FN REMOVE$ ("A caterpillar",5,8)

will print

> A car.

5.1.3 REMAIN

Function 5.3 returns the characters in X$ after position X.

```
10 DEF FN REMAIN$(X$,X)=RIGHT$(X$,LEN(X$)-X)
```

Function 5.3 REMAIN

Example:

```
10 W$="SALES : 435.44"
20 FOR I=1 TO LEN(W$):
    X$=MID$(W$,I,1):
    IF X$>="0" AND X$<="9"
        THEN
            40
30 NEXT
40 PRINT VAL(FN REMAIN$(W$,I))*2
```

will print

> 870.88.

5.1.4 STRING OF A NUMBER

Function 5.4 returns the string form of the number X, without the initial space or sign returned by STR$.

```
10 DEF FN NUM.STR$(X)=RIGHT$(STR$(X),LEN(STR$(X))-1)
```

Function 5.4 String of a number

Example:

> PRINT "*";FN NUM.STR$ (145) ;"*","*";STR$ (145) ;"*"

will print

> *145*   * 145*

5.1.5 VIEW

Function VIEW returns the character at memory position X. It is particularly useful to examine parts of the memory.

```
10 DEF FN VIEW$(X)=CHR$(PEEK(X))
```

Function 5.5 VIEW

Example:

```
10 FOR I = 41000 TO 41500:
    PRINT FN VIEW$(I);:
   NEXT
```

will print the contents of memory locations 41,000 through 41,500.

5.1.6 CURSOR RETURN

Function 5.6 returns a string that, when printed, will reproduce the string passed as argument, but will leave the cursor at the first character instead of the last. CTRL.H$ must be initialized to CHR$(8) before the actual function call.

```
10 DEF FN CUR.RET$(X$)=X$+STRING$(LEN(X$),CTRL.H$)
```

Function 5.6 CURSOR RETURN

Example:

```
PRINT FN CUR.RET$("Golden Slumbers");:W$ = INPUT$(1)
```

will print

G̲olden Slumbers.

(The underline indicates the cursor position.)

5.2 FUNCTIONS THAT MAKE DECISIONS

One of the apparent limitations of user-defined functions is that they can only be one line long, which at first sight prohibits the use of IF . . THEN ELSE statements and makes a function as simple as ABS(X) impossible to define. However, there is a way to make a function decide between two or more options (equivalent to IF . . THEN ELSE IF . . THEN ELSE IF . . to any level). In this section we will explain Boolean functions first, then functions with two options, and finally multidecision functions.

5.2.1 BOOLEAN FUNCTIONS

Boolean functions return one of two possible values, TRUE or FALSE, and can therefore be used directly in IF . . THEN statements.

Their form is

IF FN FOO(parameters)

   THEN . .

   (ELSE . .)

where FOO is the name of the Boolean function. (See Section 7.2 for a discussion of Boolean values.)

BASIC-80 has one predefined Boolean function, EOF(X), which returns FALSE if the end of the file X has not been reached, and TRUE otherwise.

Suppose you wanted your program to get the current date and check whether the day and month were valid calendar entries. One way to do this is shown in Program Fragment 5.2.

```
10 INPUT"Month : ";MONTH:
   IF MONTH<1 OR MONTH>12
      THEN
         10
20 INPUT"Day : ";DAY:
   IF DAY<1 OR DAY>31
     THEN
        20
```

Program Fragment 5.2 Checking month and day

A more flexible solution, using functions, is given in Program Fragment 5.3.

```
10 DEF FN INVALID.MONTH(X)=(X<1 OR X>12):
   DEF FN INVALID.DAY(X)=(X<1 OR X>31)
20 INPUT"MONTH ";MONTH:
   IF FN INVALID.MONTH(MONTH)
      THEN
         20
30 INPUT"DAY ";DAY:
   IF FN INVALID.DAY(DAY)
      THEN
        30
```

Program Fragment 5.3 Checking month and day with functions

Function INVALID.MONTH returns TRUE when the parameter is not a valid month number, that is, when it is either smaller than 1 or greater than 12; otherwise, it returns FALSE.[1] Likewise, function

---

[1]In BASIC, TRUE is usually considered to be − 1 and FALSE 0, and all logical operations return − 1 as TRUE. However, any nonzero value is interpreted as TRUE.

INVALID.DAY returns TRUE when the parameter is not a legal day, and FALSE otherwise. If you had to ask for several dates in different parts of your program, you would have to use a subroutine (which can be difficult to follow) or write the same program lines many times. An alternative way to write these two functions is shown in Program Fragment 5.4.

```
10 DEF FN MONTH(X)=NOT (X>=1 AND X<=12):
   DEF FN DAY(X)= NOT (X>=1 AND X<=31)
```

Program Fragment 5.4 Functions using NOT

Here is another example. You have a menu with five options, and you are going to make a choice with an INPUT$(1). A function to check whether the answer is valid is shown in Program Fragment 5.5.

```
10 DEF FN VALID(X$)=(X$>="1" AND X$<="5")
20 PRINT (MENU OPTIONS )
30 W$=INPUT$(1):
   IF FN VALID(W$)
     THEN
       ON VAL(W$) GOTO OPTION 1, OPTION 2,0!0!
     ELSE
       30
```

Program Fragment 5.5 Function valid

Notice that we are using two different types in the same function: the parameter is a string, and the function returns a Boolean. To make this function more flexible, an additional parameter can be used to signal the number of options on the menu. Function 5.7 illustrates this alternative.

```
10 DEF FN VALID(X$,Y)=(X$>="1" AND X$<=CHR$(Y+ASC("0")))
```

Function 5.7 Function valid

Notice that to compare X$ to the highest-numbered option, instead of using the STR$ function to get the string equivalent of X (which always leaves an initial space to make room for the plus sign preceding positive numbers), we used the CHR$ function, adding the ASCII of zero to Y. (That way, if $Y = 0$, CHR$$(0 + ASC("0")) = "0"$; if $Y = 1$, CHR$$(. .) = "1"$; and so forth. This is shorter than using STR$ and also easier to visualize.) An alternative would be to use the function described in Section 5.1.4.

Function 5.8a illustrates another useful device. The function returns TRUE if the parameter is even, FALSE otherwise. Using the operator NOT, we get the function ODD, Function 5.8b.

```
a - 10 DEF FN EVEN(X)=(X MOD 2 = 0)
b - 20 DEF FN ODD(X)=NOT FN EVEN(X)
```

Function 5.8 EVEN and ODD

Function 5.9 returns TRUE if X is a leap year, FALSE otherwise. A year is a leap year if it is divisible by four but not divisible by 100, or if it is divisible by both 100 and 400.

```
10 DEF FN LEAP(X)=(X MOD 4=0 AND NOT X MOD 100=0) OR
                  (X MOD 100=0 AND X MOD 400=0)
```

Function 5.9 Leap year

We next look at a function that will accept a date in string form and return TRUE if the date is valid, FALSE otherwise. The format of the string must be (MM/DD/YY), where MM is a two-digit number that indicates the month, DD the day, and YY the year, which will have to be greater than 75. In Function 5.10, we can see that to check for the validity of every number, we must enforce the format of the date, or else the string comparisons will not work. The last operation of the function definition checks whether the length is correct and returns FALSE when X$ has fewer or more than eight characters. Notice that there are four AND operators (two of which are composed of two AND's). This means that if at least one subexpression is FALSE, the whole expression will be FALSE.

```
5 DEF FN VALID.DATE(X$)=(LEFT$(X$,2)>"01" AND LEFT$(X$,2)<="12")
               AND (MID$(X$,4,2)>="01" AND MID$(X$,4,2)<="31")
               AND (RIGHT$(X$,2)>"75") AND LEN(X$)=8
```

Function 5.10 Valid date

If you had to verify many dates at different points in your program, mentioned earlier, a subroutine could be used, but would never be as clear as saying

IF VALID.DATE(TODAY$) THEN . . .

after the function is defined.

Boolean functions can be used for relatively elaborate comparisons. In the following sections we will see several examples of their use.

5.2.2 TWO-WAY DECISIONS

A common and useful function with a two-way decision is MAX(X,Y) which returns the larger of X and Y. Normally, an IF . .

THEN ELSE statement (IF X☐Y THEN (return X) ELSE (return Y)) would be necessary. However, using Boolean values, we can make the decision directly.

If we perform the Boolean operation (X>Y), we get −1 if X is greater than Y, zero otherwise. If we multiply the resulting number by X (for example, (12>3)*12), we will get −X (−12 in the example), which is −1 times X, or zero when X<Y. On the other hand, if we perform ((Y>X)*Y), we get −Y when Y>X, zero otherwise. If we now add the two parts ((X>Y)*X + (Y>X)*Y), we get −X when X>Y, Y when Y>X. We now need only to multiply the result by −1 to get the correct result. The final version can be seen in Function 5.11.

```
10 DEF FN MAX(X,Y)=-((X>Y)*X+(Y>X)*Y)
```

Function 5.11 Maximum of two numbers

The definition of the function MINIMUM is left as an exercise.

A similar technique can be used to force decisions when dealing with a string. Of course, a string cannot be multiplied by FALSE or TRUE, but a comparable effect can be produced if LEFT$ or RIGHT$ is used: when the numeric argument of either of these functions is zero, the null string is returned, and when the argument is positive, the length of the string returned is the minimum of the argument and the length of the original string. Let's look at Program Fragment 5.6:

```
10 INPUT"Length : ";LENGTH
20 PRINT LEFT$("STROGANOFF",LENGTH):GOTO 10
```

Program Fragment 5.6 Chopping off characters with LEFT$

If you type 0, no characters are returned. If you type a number smaller than the length of "STROGANOFF" (4, for example), that number of characters is returned ("STRO" in the example). If you type a number greater than the length of "STROGANOFF" (35, for example), only those characters available will be returned (the entire string, "STROGANOFF").

Now we can use the Boolean values to produce the numerical argument of LEFT$ or RIGHT$. If the value is FALSE (0), no characters are returned, which is the equivalent of the FALSE string. If the value is TRUE (−1) and we multiply it by a negative number,[2] the result is positive and can be used as the argument of LEFT$ to return the desired string.

---

[2]Usually a number whose ABSolute value is greater than the length of the string argument of LEFT$ will be a good choice. However, if you want your function to return a string of fixed length, a specific number must be used.

Function 5.12 returns the strings "TRUE" or "FALSE" according to the Boolean value used as argument. The Boolean values are multiplied by −5 to guarantee that the string returned is five characters long.

```
10 DEF FN BOOL$(X)=LEFT$("TRUE ",(X = -1)*-5) +
               LEFT$("FALSE",(X = 0)*-5)
```

Function 5.12 String Boolean

5.2.3 MULTIPLE-WAY DECISIONS

Boolean values can be used to make a decision between many options in a way equivalent to the chain

IF .. THEN .. ELSE IF .. THEN ... etc.

Function 5.13 returns the day of the week spelled out. Therefore, it has to decide whether the argument is equal to 1 for Monday, 2 for Tuesday, and so forth. Function A in line 10 was defined to produce the desired length (9 if X = Y, 0 otherwise) and to make the definition of DAY$ clearer. Notice that when function A is invoked, no space is left between FN and A. This is perfectly valid.

```
10 DEF FN A(X,Y)=-9*(X=Y)
20 DEF FN DAY$(X)=LEFT$("Monday   ",FNA(X,1))+
               LEFT$("Tuesday  ",FNA(X,2))+
               LEFT$("Wednesday",FNA(X,3))+
               LEFT$("Thursday ",FNA(X,4))+
               LEFT$("Friday   ",FNA(X,5))+
               LEFT$("Saturday ",FNA(X,6))+
               LEFT$("Sunday   ",FNA(X,7))
```

Function 5.13 Day of the week spelled out

5.3 DEFINING ERRORS

Most of the predefined functions produce an error when invalid parameters are used. LEFT$, for example, will print 'illegal function call' when its argument is either negative or greater than 255. Since we can now make decisions within the function declaration, we can include a part that will produce an error upon finding invalid parameters. Suppose we want to make sure that the argument used in the invocation of function DAY$ (see Function 5.12) is valid. There are three cases that could be considered invalid: a number smaller than 1, a number greater than 7, and a fractional number. Given the definitions of Function 5.13, the additional line shown in Function 5.14 will check for these 'illegal parameter' cases.

```
30 DEF FN CHECKED.DAY$(X)=FN DAY$ + LEFT$("",X < 1) +
            LEFT$("",X > 7) + LEFT$("",INT(X)<>X)
```

Function 5.14 Checked DAY

If the three comparisons are FALSE (which means that the argument is valid), three null strings are added to the name of the day returned by FN DAY$, leaving it unmodified. If at least one of the comparisons yields a TRUE, the function tries to evaluate LEFT$ with a negative argument, and this causes an 'illegal function call' message to be printed with the line number where the function was invoked, not the line number where the evaluation actually took place.

If an error-checking part must be added to a numerical function, you can convert the LEFT$ part (you can use RIGHT$, too, or any other string function that will cause an error with a negative argument) to a number with the VAL function. If no error is caused, a zero will be added to the other values, having no effect. An alternative method is to use a numerical function, such as PEEK, that causes an error with a negative argument. However, the value returned by the function should be multiplied by zero in order to preserve the value of the original function. (PEEK(0) is not necessarily zero.)

Functon 5.15 returns TRUE if the argument is even, FALSE otherwise. It checks whether the argument is an integer number. If it is, the function LEFT$ returns a null string which becomes zero with VAL. If the number is not an integer, the attempt to evaluate LEFT$ with -1 as argument causes an 'illegal function call'.

```
10 DEF FN EVEN.CHECK(X)=(X MOD 2=0)+VAL(LEFT$("",X<>INT(X)))
```

Function 5.15 Checked EVEN

5.4 NUMERICAL FUNCTIONS

The BASIC manual lists in an appendix a number of the most commonly used mathematical functions. In this section we will discuss some useful nonstandard numerical functions.

5.4.1 FUNCTION RANDOM

The function RND returns a value between 0 and 1 without actually reaching 1 (0 <= RND < 1), but many times what you need is an integer between 1 and a certain upper limit (as in FOR loops or to index arrays). Function 5.16 returns an integer between 1 and the parameter provided.

```
10 DEF FN RAN(X)=1+INT(X*RND)
```

Function 5.16 Integer random

The RND function returns up to 6 digits. Function 5.17 returns a double-precision random number between 0 and 1 with up to 12 significant digits. The argument X is not used in the computation, so any number or valid expression can be used.

```
10 DEF FN RANDOM#(X)=RND+RND/1E+06
```

Function 5.17 Double-precision random

5.4.2 MOD AND DIV

The operators " \ " and MOD work only with integers. Functions 5.18a and 5.18b perform the same operations on single- and double-precision numbers.

```
a - 10 DEF FN DIV(X,Y)=INT(X/Y):
       DEF FN MODULO(X,Y)=X-Y*FN DIV(X,Y)

B - 10 DEF FN DIV#(X#,Y#)=INT(X#/Y#):
       DEF FN MODULO#(X#,Y#)=X#-Y#*FN DIV#(X#,Y#)
```

Function 5.18 DIV and MODulo

5.4.3 NUMBER OF DAYS IN THE MONTH

Here is an example of a function that must make a complicated choice: given a number from 1 to 12, return the number of days in the month denoted by that number. The simple way to do it would be to say "If the argument is 1, return 31; if it is 2, return 28; . . .", but that would be a long and not very interesting function. We will derive a more general function.

If we forget temporarily about the only anomalous month, namely, February, the months can be split into two kinds:

I   Up to 7:   If the number is even, number of days = 30.
             If number is odd, number of days = 31.
II Above 7: If number is even, number of days = 31.
             If number is odd, number of days = 30.

Since the difference between the two is only one day, we can start with a base of 30 days and add 0 or 1, depending on whether condition I or II obtains. This can be easily implemented with the help of the functions ODD and EVEN:

FN DAYS(X) = 30 + (X<8)*FN ODD(X) + (X>7)*FN EVEN(X)

So far, everything is fine, except that February returns 30 days, so we must add a part that subtracts 2 from the rest of the expression when the argument is 2. This part is *simply* 2*(X = 2). Now we add a little error checking and the function is ready:

```
10 DEF FN DAYS(X)=30+(X<8)*FN ODD(X)+(X>7)*FN EVEN(X)+
      2*(X=2)+VAL(LEFT$("",X<1 OR X>12 OR X<>INT(X)))
```

Function 5.19 Number of days in the month

5.5 DEFINING NEW DATA TYPES

The type *single precision* is really a subset of *double precision*. (Every single-precision value can be stored in a double-precision variable.) The type *integer* is a subset of *single precision*, and the type *Boolean* is a subset of *integer*.

Many times, you want to handle considerably fewer values than those of the types already available, and you do not want to waste memory (or disk) space. If so, you can define your own data types, as long as they are representable in some of the variables available in BASIC. Functions give you the ideal tool to do this with, and even to check for inclusion in the new type range. We will examine some examples of nonstandard data types, but it is really up to you to create your own, according to your own personal needs.

5.5.1 UNSIGNED INTEGERS

Standard integers occupy two bytes and in theory could handle values from 0 to 65,536. Because negative numbers are allowed, the whole range is shifted, and the resulting range is from $-32,768$ to 32,767. When you are only going to use positive integers, and you need the extra values, Functions 5.20a and 5.20b are very easy ways to give you what you want.

```
a - 10 DEF FN USINT%(X)=X-32768!       (Encode)

b - 10 DEF FN VALUS(X%)=X%+32768!      (Decode)
```

Function 5.20 Unsigned integers

5.5.2 SHORT INTEGERS

Every byte can store values from zero to 255. If this range is sufficient for your application, you can easily work with bytes by means of the functions CHR$(X) and ASC("X"), using strings to store your short integers. Since a byte is the same size as a character, every string variable can be used to store up to 255 of these short integers. Program Fragment 5.7 uses only two string variables to simulate an array with 510 variables of type short integer. The two functions calculate the position of the character in the array (FN INDEX) and in the string (FN CHAR).

```
10 '
                      ** SHORT **
             Type short integer (one byte)

20 DIM A$(1):HOME:
   FOR I=0 TO 1:
     A$(I)=STRING$(255,0):
   NEXT
30 DEF FN INDEX(X)=INT((X-1)/255):
   DEF FN CHAR(X)=INT((X-1) MOD 255)+1
40 INPUT"POSITION (1-510) ";POSITION
50 INPUT"1-STORE, 2-RECALL";MODE:
   ON MODE GOTO 60,80
60 INPUT"Value (0-255) ";VALUE
70 MID$(A$(FN INDEX(POSITION)),
              FN CHAR(POSITION),1)=
                          CHR$(VALUE):GOTO 40
80 W=ASC(MID$(A$(FN INDEX(POSITION)),
                    FN CHAR(POSITION),1)):
   PRINT W:GOTO 40
1000 WHILE -1:
       INPUT W:PRINT FN INDEX(W)" "FN CHAR(W):
     WEND
```

Program Fragment 5.7

5.5.3 BIT BOOLEAN VARIABLES

When space is crucial, you want to save every possible bit. Every byte contains eight bits, each one of which can take two values: zero or one (which can represent TRUE or FALSE, open or closed, on or off, or any two-state condition). You can consider a byte as an array of eight bits, and therefore one string variable can store an array of 2040 bits! In Program Fragment 5.8, function SET sets a particular bit in a byte (stores a one in it), and function UNSET resets it (stores a zero in it). Function SCAN returns the current Boolean value of the Xth bit of a particular byte.

(For a more complete discussion of bits and bytes, see Section 7.1.)

O ·

```
          ** BIT **
       Operations at bit level

10 DEF FN SET(BYTE,BIT)=PEEK(BYTE) OR 2^BIT
20 DEF FN UNSET(BYTE,BIT)=PEEK(BYTE) AND NOT 2^BIT
30 DEF FN SCAN(BYTE,BIT)=(PEEK(BYTE) AND 2^BIT)<>0
40 W=0:R=0:I=0:X=0:X=VARPTR(W):POKE X,0
50 INPUT"BIT ";BIT:
   INPUT"1-SET, 2-RESET, 3-SCAN ";R
60 ON R GOTO 70,80,90
70 POKE X,FN SET(X,BIT):GOTO 50
80 POKE X,FN UNSET(X,BIT):GOTO 50
90 IF FN SCAN(X,BIT)
      THEN
        PRINT"ON"
      ELSE
        PRINT"OFF"
100 GOTO 50
```

Program Fragment 5.8

Exercises

1. Write a function that returns the minimum of at least three numbers (FN MINIMUM(X,Y,Z, . . .)).

2. Write a function that spells the names of the months of the year, all with a common length. (This is not as straightforward as it seems.)

3. Write a functon that returns the factorial of its argument, for numbers 0 through 5.

4. We want to define a new data type, the integers from 1 to 15. Write two functions, PRED(X) and SUCC(X), that will return the predecessor and successor of the argument X in this new data type. As an example, PRED(5) = 4, but PRED(1) = 15; SUCC(9) = 10, but SUCC(15) = 1.

5. A collection of numbers is in string form, but some have non-numeric characters to the left or right, so VAL cannot be used. All the numbers start with a "0" (e.g., "Bruja0123.5U", "*0500.45Arepa"). Write a function that returns the value of the embedded numbers. (Hint: the position of the number can be found with INSTR.)

6. The 'sieve of Eratosthenes' is a very short and fast algorithm to find prime numbers using an array to store 1's or 0's. Here is a version using an array of integers:

```
10 INPUT N:DIM M%(N):TRUE=-1
20 FOR I%=2 TO SQR(N):
       IF NOT M%(I%)
          THEN
             PRINT I%;:
             FOR J%=2*I% TO N STEP I%:
               M%(J%)=TRUE:
             NEXT
30 NEXT
40 FOR J%=I% TO N:
       IF NOT M%(J%)
          THEN
             PRINT J%;
50 NEXT
```

Change the program, using an array of bits (which can be stored in strings or numeric arrays.) You should be able to calculate the prime numbers up to at least 150,000.

7. Modify Function 5.19 so that it takes not only the month, but also the year as arguments, and returns 29 when the month is February and the year is a leap year.

POINTERS

6

The concept of pointers is one of the most powerful and least publicized in BASIC. Though used extensively in other languages (such as PASCAL and C), it has not been well documented in BASIC, and therefore very few applications use it. Unlike the concepts described in the previous chapters, pointers do not make a program more understandable, but their capabilities warrant inclusion in this book.

6.1 NUMERICAL POINTERS

When a variable is used for the first time in a program, BASIC stores its name in a special list, along with some additional information such as the type of the variable, whether it is array or not, and, most important of all, the address in memory where the actual contents of the variable are placed. This address is returned by the function VARPTR. To access the variables through their address, you must remember that the internal representation of numbers can be decoded with the help of CVI, CVS, and CVD, and that the encoding can be achieved with MKI$, MKS$, and MKD$. Consider an example. Program 6.1 initializes the variables I, J, X, and X$ in line 10:

```
10 I=0:J=0:X=0:X$=""
20 INPUT I:X=VARPTR(I)
30 FOR J=0 TO 3:
       X$=X$+CHR$(PEEK(X+J)):
   NEXT
40 PRINT CVS(X$):X$="":GOTO 20
```

Program 6.1

In line 30, X$ gets a copy of the internal representation of I, since the address of its four bytes (the number of bytes of a single-precision number) is located with VARPTR. The program then gets the value of I without using its name in any way: There is no reference to I in lines 30 or 40. The process is shown in Figure 6.1

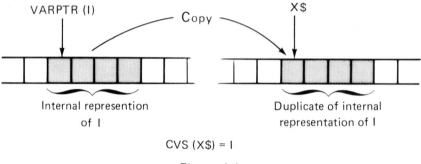

CVS (X$) = I

Figure 6.1

The initializations in line 10 are necessary[1] because if, after getting the pointer to I in line 20, we used J, for example, its allocation in the variable list might make I change address in memory, and X would end up pointing to an address in memory that no longer contains I.

6.1.1 REFERENCED VARIABLES

One of the conveniences of a user-defined function is the possibility of calling it with different variables. A regular subroutine, by contrast, can only use values passed to it through fixed variables and is therefore much less flexible: if you want to transfer a subroutine from one program to another, you must use the same variable names or edit the subroutine.

As shown in Program 6.1, pointers allow you to get the value of a variable using only its address, and not its name. Program Fragment

---

[1]When new variables are used, they can displace the position of the old ones. Thus, you should initialize all the variables you intend to use before handling pointers.

6.2 prints the numbers from 1 to the number passed as parameter. Notice that lines 20 and 30 call subroutine 500 with the addresses of J% and K% and that the subroutine does not make use of J% or K% at all. It does not even have to know which variables are being used! Since J% and K% are integers, line 500 must move only two bytes. Instead of using MKI% to get the values of the variables whose addresses are sent to the subroutine, the internal representations of those values are copied into the variable TEMP, which can now be used as if it were the original.

```
10 I=0:J=0:X=0:Y=0:TEMP=0
20 INPUT J:X=VARPTR(J):GOSUB 500
30 INPUT K:X=VARPTR(K):GOSUB 500:GOTO 20
500 Y=VARPTR(TEMP):
    FOR I=0 TO 1:
      POKE Y+I,PEEK(X+I):
    NEXT
510 FOR I=1 TO TEMP:
      PRINT CHR$(13);I;:
    NEXT:
    PRINT:RETURN
```

Program 6.2

Program 6.3 inputs values into one-dimensional arrays whose dimensions are passed as pointers. Line 20 calls subroutine 1000 to do the input of M( ), and line 30 calls it once more to enter T( ).

```
0 '
                    ** ARRAYINP **
           Input of array through pointers.

10 OPTION BASE 1:INPUT"N=";N:INPUT"M=";M:
   DIM M(N),T(M):I=0:J=0:W=0:X=0:Y=0:Z=0:
   VALUE=0:NUM.EL=0
20 Y=VARPTR(N):X=VARPTR(M(1)):GOSUB 1000
30 Y=VARPTR(M):X=VARPTR(T(1)):GOSUB 1000
40 FOR I=1 TO N:
     PRINT M(I);:
   NEXT:PRINT:
   FOR I=1 TO M:
     PRINT T(I);:
   NEXT:
   END

50 FOR I=0 TO N:
     PRINT M(I);:
   NEXT:PRINT:
   FOR I=0 TO M:
     PRINT P(I);:
   NEXT:
   END
```

```
1000 Z=VARPTR(NUM.EL):
     FOR I=0 TO 3:
       POKE Z+I,PEEK(Y+I):
     NEXT:
     W=VARPTR(VALUE)
1010 FOR I=1 TO NUM.EL:
     PRINT"(";I;")=";:INPUT VALUE:
     FOR J=0 TO 3:
       POKE X+J,PEEK(W+J):
     NEXT
1020  X=X+4:
     NEXT:
     RETURN
```

Program 6.3

6.1.2 CHANGING THE REFERENCED VARIABLES

Since we know exactly where in memory to find a specific variable, we cannot only get its value, but also change its contents.

Program 6.3 inputs a single-precision number from the keyboard and returns it in the variable whose address is set in X. The subroutine cannot only be called from anywhere in the program, but it can be called for any variable. As with Program 6.2, the subroutine does not have to know which variable is being used, as long as it is of the same type, single precision in this case.

```
0  '
                        ** Referenced variable **

10 I=0:X=0:Y=0:VALUE=0:TEMP=0
20 X=VARPTR(VALUE):GOSUB 1000:PRINT VALUE
30 X=VARPTR(COST):GOSUB 1000:PRINT COST:GOTO 20
1000 INPUT TEMP:Y=VARPTR(TEMP):
     FOR I=0 TO 3:
       POKE X+I,PEEK(Y+I):
     NEXT:RETURN
```

Program 6.4

Notice that there is no way to accomplish the action of subroutine 1000 with a function.

6.1.3 ARRAY MANIPULATION WITH POINTERS

Arrays are stored sequentially in memory as described in Section 4.2.2. Since the address of every element is a function of the DIMensions and of the type (an array of integers will use two bytes per element, whereas one of double precision will take eight), a single pointer is sufficient to determine the address of any element of the array. The array begins in the first element, the one with all indices equal to 1.[2] In this first example we will assume that N and M are global variables, that is, that their values contain the number of columns and rows in an array and are sent not as pointers, but as regular variables. Program 6.5 does the input of a two-dimensional array of integers. Since N and M are global, they must be changed every time you want to work with a different array. A more flexible method will be studied later.

```
0 ' ** 2-D Array input **
5 HOME
10 DEF FN POSITION(I,J)=(J-1)*N+I
20 OPTION BASE 1:N=5:M=3:
    DIM M%(N,M):
    I=0:J=0:W=0:X=0:Y=0:Z=0:K=0:VALUE%=0
30 X=VARPTR(M%(1,1)):GOSUB 1000
40 FOR I=1 TO N:
    FOR J=1 TO M:
        PRINT M%(I,J);:
    NEXT:PRINT:
    NEXT
50 END
1000 W=VARPTR(VALUE%)
1010 FOR I=1 TO N:
    FOR J=1 TO M
1011    PRINT"M("I","J")=";:
        INPUT VALUE%
1012    Z=(FN POSITION(I,J)-1)*2
1015    FOR K=0 TO 1:
            POKE X+Z+K,PEEK(W+K):
        NEXT
1020    NEXT:
    NEXT:
    RETURN
```

Program 6.5

6.1.4 PASSING MORE THAN ONE ADDRESS AS PARAMETER

Program 6.5 is static because it needs the sizes of the array in a specific variable, N. To make the input subroutine more general (so that it can be stored and added to any program for immediate use), the value of N (and M, if the array is three-dimensional) must be sent as an address. The easiest way to do this is to use two variables. An alter-

---

[2]We assume that OPTION BASE is set to 1 to facilitate the calculations.

native way is to use X (or the variable which is used to send the address) to transfer two addresses. X is a single-precision variable, so it uses four bytes. But only two bytes are needed to store an address of up to 64 K, so we can use one single-precision variable to store two addresses. Let's see how it is done. We want to store the two addresses 23,500 and 43,671 in one single-precision variable. Since every byte can store values from 0 to 255, we must take each address and reduce it to two bytes. We will use the functions defined in Section 5.4.2, because " \ " and MOD only work with integers, and addresses greater than 32,767 cannot be handled by these operators.

Let's start with 23,500:

FN DIV(23500,256) = 91   (Equivalent to INT(23500/256) = 91)

FN MODULO(23500,256) = 204

The low byte is, then, 204, the high byte, 91. Now for 43,671, we have

    FN DIV(43671,256) = 170

    FN MODULO(43671,256) = 151

Thus,

    X = CVS(CHR$(204) + CHR$(91) + CHR$(151) + CHR$(170))

To restore the values once inside the subroutine, we simply execute

```
1000 X$=MKS$(X):
     ADDRESS1=ASC(LEFT$(X$,1))+256*ASC(MID$(X$,2,1)):
     ADDRESS2=ASC(MID$(X$,3,1))+256*ASC(RIGHT$(X$,1))
```

The same method can be used to send four addresses in a double-precision variable. In the next few sections we will study some useful concepts related to this 'packing' of numbers.

6.1.5 MULTIPLE-TYPE SUBROUTINES

Program 6.6 does input for all three types of numeric variables, using the contents of TYPE (which can be either integer (1), single precision (2), or double precision (3)) to select the type, and returns the value in the appropriate variable.

```
10 '
                    ** ALLTYPES **
          Storage of the three types in string var.

15 HOME
20 PRINT"1-STORE, 2-RECALL ";
30 W$=INPUT$(1):
   IF W$="2"
       THEN
           70
```

```
        ELSE
            IF W$<>"1"
                THEN
                    30
                ELSE
    40              PRINT:INPUT"VALUE ";VALUE$:GOSUB 500:
                    ON TYPE GOTO 42,44,46
    42 A$=MKI$(VAL(VALUE$)):GOTO 20
    44 A$=MKS$(VAL(VALUE$)):GOTO 20
    46 A$=MKD$(VAL(VALUE$)):GOTO 20
    70 IF LEN(A$)=2
        THEN
            S$=STR$(CVI(A$))
        ELSE
            IF LEN(A$)=4
                THEN
                    S$=STR$(CVS(A$))
                ELSE
                    S$=STR$(CVD(A$))
    80 PRINT S$:GOTO 20
    500 PRINT:PRINT"1-INTEGER":
        PRINT"2-SINGLE PRECISION":
        PRINT"3-DOUBLE PRECISION ";
    510 W$=INPUT$(1):
        IF W$<"1" OR W$>"3"
            THEN
                510
            ELSE
                TYPE=VAL(W$):PRINT:RETURN
```

Program 6.6

6.2 STRING POINTERS

Since strings do not have a fixed length, pointers to them are different from pointers to numeric variables. The address returned by VARPTR points to the 'string descriptor block', a group of three bytes with the following meaning:

Byte 1 (VARPTR)   = current length of the string.

Byte 2 (VARPTR + 1) = Least significant byte of the real address.

Byte 3 (VARPTR + 2) = Most significant byte of the real address.

To get the real address, a small calculation must be performed. Suppose, for example, VARPTR returned the number 25,698. Then the real address is given by

PEEK(25699) + 256*PEEK(25700),

In general, if X = VARPTR(⟨string⟩), then the real address of the string is

PEEK(X + 1) + 256*PEEK(X + 2).

6.2.1 CHANGING A STRING'S LENGTH

Knowing that the length of any string is in the address returned by VARPTR, we can easily change it by POKEing different values into this location. Program 6.7 reduces the length of A$ in every loop, without really changing A$. At the end, the original length is POKEd back in, and A$ remains unchanged.

```
10 A$="Tintin":I=0:X=0:L=0
20 X=VARPTR(A$):L=PEEK(X)
30 FOR I=1 TO LEN(A$):
       POKE X,L-1:PRINT A$:
   NEXT
40 POKE X,L
```

Program 6.7

6.2.2 REDIRECTING STRINGS

Since we now know where the address of any string resides, we can change it by POKEing into it different values, to 'fool' BASIC into believing that the string is really elsewhere. Program 6.8 changes the length and address of string A$, so that it becomes a copy of B$. (It really is B$ until it is changed.)

```
10 X=0:Y=0:I=0:A$=""
20 INPUT B$
30 X=VARPTR(A$):Y=VARPTR(B$)
40 FOR I=0 TO 2:
       POKE X+I,PEEK(Y+I):
   NEXT
50 PRINT A$
```

Program 6.8

Though A$ is really B$ after line 40, as soon as B$ is changed in any way, it is placed in a new address. A$ will still have the previous contents of B$, but B$ will now be different. This change of address is necessary because of the changing lengths of strings.

6.2.3 MIXING TYPES

In the discussion about the MKx$ and CVx functions (Section 4.2), we saw that a numeric variable can be considered to be a string with a special format. If you redirect a string (by changing its address) and make it point to a numeric variable, it will contain the MKx$ of the value of the variable. (The length must be adjusted also, to make it correspond to the type of the numeric variable.) Program 6.9 changes the pointers of V$ so that it becomes an 'alias' for the numeric variable VALUE. Since the positon of numeric variables does not change as randomly as that of strings, once V$ points to VALUE, it remains that way until the introduction of a new variable makes it move.

```
10 I=0:X=0:VALUE=0
20 X=VARPTR(V$):Y=VARPTR(VALUE):POKE X,4:
   POKE X+1,Y MOD 256:POKE X+2,Y \ 256
30 INPUT VALUE
40 PRINT CVS(V$):GOTO 30
```

Program 6.9

6.2.4 REFERENCING STRINGS

If you send the address of a string as the parameter of a subroutine, it is easy to get the contents of the string into a local (or at least locally used) variable that can be used to store the strings that result from the intermediate calculations. When the process is finished, the address and length of the resulting string can be found by means of VARPTR and POKEd into the string descriptor block of the original string so that the only element moved are its pointers. An alternative way of passing the resulting string to the calling one is to do the transfer with LSET (or RSET) and set the length of the calling string accordingly. This, however, can be done only when the calling string is at least as long as the resulting one. If the string transferred is shorter than the original one, LSET adds spaces to the resulting string to keep the length unchanged.

6.2.5 STORING DATA
IN THE PROGRAM BODY

When a string is assigned to a string variable in a line of a program, the address found in the string descriptor block is the part of the program where the assignment is made; that is, the string is found in the program and is not transferred to string memory until it is changed in some way. Any attempt to modify the string causes it to be copied in string memory to protect the program. (This is the only case in which even LSET and RSET cause a movement of the string.) In Figure 6.2 the address of A$ returned by VARPTR is shown with an arrow.

```
10 A$="Peter and the wolf"
        ↑
```
Figure 6.2 Address of a constant string

To force a string that is assigned inside the program body to be copied to string space (and thus take the string address out of your program), add +" " as shown in Example 6.1.

10 A$ = "Peter and the wolf" + " ".

6.2.5.1 Adding Special Characters to Lines of a Program

There are some special characters that cannot be included in any line of a program because they have special meaning for BASIC. One example is the carriage return (CHR$(13) or Ctrl-M); it cannot be entered normally in a line of a program because it is used to terminate input. Another example is the backspace (CHR$(8) or Ctrl-H), which cannot be present in any program lines because of its use as an editing command. As we have seen in Section 2.5, some of these characters can have special effects on the terminal and can be used to accelerate the creation of screens. Of these characters, the only one allowed in a program line is the line feed (CHR$(10) or Ctrl-J), which moves the cursor down one line.[3]

Knowing the address of a literal (the letters inside the quotes that are assigned to a string variable), you can change it easily by means of the POKE command. Program 6.10 lets you change the contents of A$ to any characters you care to key in, except carriage return. (If carriage return is included in a line of a program, the characters following it are interpreted as a line number and produce a 'ghost' number.) Thus, you can draw an entire screen by printing this string (Program 6.8 uses only one string, so that the screen is limited to some 240 characters; if you need more space, you can use more strings), and you do not have to read the string in as input because it is readily available in the program. Of course, the number of characters POKEd into the program line cannot exceed the length originally assigned to A$ or some of these characters will erase part of the program, leading to a certain disaster.

Notice that in line 40 the line feed (Ctrl-J) is echoed followed by a carriage return, because that is the way it will be printed by BASIC.

```
O  '
                    ** ADDCTRL **  .
            Adding control characters to program

10  X=O:I=O:W$="":CTRL.J$=CHR$(10):
    CR.RET$=CHR$(13):HOME:WIDTH(254)
20  A$="

            "
30  X=VARPTR(A$):X=PEEK(X+1)+PEEK(X+2)*256:
```

---

[3]If line feed is used in a program line, its effect is not only to move the cursor to the next line down, but to move it to the left margin, too. What happens is that a carriage return is produced automatically, although it is not actually included in the line.

```
      FOR I=0 TO LEN(A$)-1
   40    W$=INPUT$(1):POKE X+I,ASC(W$):
         IF W$<>CTRL.J$
           THEN
             PRINT W$;
           ELSE
             PRINT W$;CR.RET$;
   50 NEXT
```

Program 6.10

6.2.5.2 Hiding Parts of Your Program

When you want parts of your program to be invisible to other people,[4] you can use some of the cursor movement control characters to erase the parts that you want to hide.[5] In Program 6.11 line 10 prints

20 A$ = "__

and leaves the cursor right after the quote so that you know exactly where it is when the program is LISTed. Now enter the following sequence of characters:

1. *Backspaces:* make the cursor move to the left-hand margin of the screen.
2. *Spaces:* replace the line number and the A$ = '', erasing them.

At this point, enter anything you want. Use Ctrl-C to exit the program, because the string is actually changed with every character entered. If you LIST your program now, the only thing you will see of line 20 will be the characters keyed in after the spaces. There will be no line number and no BASIC instructions—just a message floating in the middle of nowhere. And since the line number cannot be seen, superior guesswork must be done to edit it. Now it makes perfectly good sense to have a program with an introductory part like the one shown in Figure 6.3.

```
*******************************
*          Program FOO        *
*                             *
*          Written by         *
*                             *
*        Gabriel Cuellar      *
*******************************
```

Figure 6.3 Header of a program

---

[4]To make the entire program invisible to others, save it with the ''R'' option (e.g., SAVE''PROGRAM'',R). The problem is that it becomes invisible to you, too, and cannot be LISTed or edited in any way.

[5]If your terminal has a code to erase the entire screen, and you use it as the first character in a string, a LIST will clear the screen as soon as the string appears.

You can hide any part of the program merely by following it with a string assignment that is later 'planted' with erasing characters. If the last character of a line is a quote, it can be replaced by any other character; it will become part of the string and will not reveal that there is a string assignment involved. Once the line has been changed, the part of the program that took care of the modification can be deleted.

```
0 '
                        ** HIDDEN **
                    Hiding parts of the program

10 X=0:I=0:W$="":CTRL.J$=CHR$(10):
   CR.RET$=CHR$(13):HOME:WIDTH(254):PRINT:PRINT:
   PRINT:PRINT:PRINT"20 A$=";CHR$(34);
20 A$="

                           "
30 X=VARPTR(A$):X=PEEK(X+1)+PEEK(X+2)*256:
   FOR I=0 TO LEN(A$)-1
40    W$=INPUT$(1):POKE X+I,ASC(W$):
      IF W$<>CTRL.J$
         THEN
            PRINT W$;
         ELSE
            PRINT W$;CR.RET$;
50 NEXT
```

Program 6.11

6.2.6 ARRAYS OF MIXED TYPES

By means of the technique explained in Sections 6.1.4 and 6.2.3, a numeric variable can be used to store a value of a lower type. Thus, a double-precision variable can store one or two single-precision values and up to four integers. A single-precision variable can be used to store one or two integer values. A string variable, having variable length, can be used to store numeric values of any type, so that up to 31 double-precision, 63 single-precision, or 127 integer-values can be stored in it. Program 6.12 uses a string variable to store numbers of any type. Since we know how to make a string variable point to a numeric one, this same scheme can be used for real numeric variables. Another convenient use of this technique is to have a string array that is used to store values of different numeric types (even short integers).

```
10 ' ** Storage of the three types in string var **
15 HOME
20 PRINT"1-STORE, 2-RECALL ";
30 W$=INPUT$(1):
   IF W$="2"
```

```
      THEN
          70
      ELSE
          IF W$<>"1"
             THEN
                 30
             ELSE
 40              PRINT:INPUT"VALUE ";VALUE$:GOSUB 500:
                 ON TYPE GOTO 42,44,46
 42 A$=MKI$(VAL(VALUE$)):GOTO 20
 44 A$=MKS$(VAL(VALUE$)):GOTO 20
 46 A$=MKD$(VAL(VALUE$)):GOTO 20
 70 IF LEN(A$)=2
      THEN
         S$=STR$(CVI(A$))
      ELSE
         IF LEN(A$)=4
            THEN
                S$=STR$(CVS(A$))
            ELSE
                S$=STR$(CVD(A$))
 80 PRINT S$:GOTO 20
 500 PRINT:PRINT"1-INTEGER":PRINT"2-SINGLE PRECISION":
     PRINT"3-DOUBLE PRECISION ";
 510 W$=INPUT$(1):
     IF W$<"1" OR W$>"3"
        THEN
            510
        ELSE
            TYPE=VAL(W$):PRINT:RETURN
```

Program 6.12

6.2.7 PREVENTING GARBAGE COLLECTION

The use of pointers to strings has the drawback that if garbage collection[6] takes place between the moment in which the pointer is copied and the time of its actual use, the correspondence between the two is lost, and terrible things are bound to happen. The way to perform voluntary garbage collection is to use the function FRE with a string argument:

X = FRE(" ")

FRE used with a numeric argument returns the memory available for variables, without performing garbage collection. If you are going to use

---

[6]Every new assignment to a string, and every intermediate string calculation, is placed in an unused part of the memory, leaving behind all the old versions of the strings. When all of memory has been used, BASIC must perform what is called a "garbage collection," in which all the unused space is restored and the strings are compressed. In the worst cases, the process can take up to a couple of minutes.

string pointers, it is a good idea to check, by means of FRE, whether garbage collection might occur soon (when BASIC runs out of memory), as shown in Subroutine 6.1. If there are fewer than 400 bytes available (the number is completely arbitrary—if you want to be extra careful, you might use a bigger number), a garbage collection is forced.

```
1000 IF FRE(1)<400
        THEN
            X=FRE("")
1010 RETURN
```

Subroutine 6.1 Voluntary garbage collection

6.2.8 MOVING ARRAYS IN MEMORY

When you have a string of 255 characters and copy it into another string, it takes BASIC nearly the same time as when you move a numeric variable, because the real delay of every instruction is all the bookkeeping and checking before its actual execution. If you have to move an array of 127 integers, for example, you must execute at least 127 instructions plus the comparisons in the corresponding loop. To move an equivalent amount of data in string form, one instruction is enough. Making use of our knowledge to redirect strings in memory, we can change the pointer of a string and make it point to the first element of a numeric array. If we have a second array of the same size, another string variable will let us copy the first string directly, so that the numeric array will be copied with a single instruction.

Let's look at the process graphically. Figure 6.4 shows an array in its sequential representation. The string A$ is redirected and forced to point

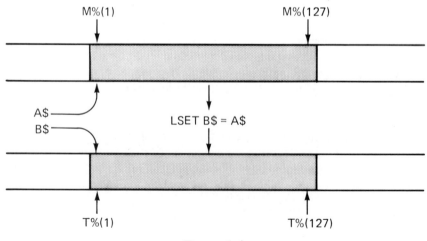

Figure 6.4

to M%(1). A second array, T% is the same size as M%, and B$ is made to point to T%(1). Using LSET to copy A$ into B$, the entire M% is copied into T% with only one command.

Notice the use of LSET. If you had used a regular assignment statement to copy one string into another, the resulting string would be placed in a new location in memory, and the numbers would not end up in the desired place. LSET and RSET will always copy a string without changing the address of the destination string. This is so because the length of the destination string is not affected, as we have seen in Section 4.2. That is why LSET and RSET are used to move strings into the disk buffers, whose location is fixed. The only case in which the resulting string is moved is when the destination is still in program memory, as explained in Section 6.2.5.

This method can be used to move numeric arrays of any type. Since the number of possible ways in which you may move the elements of an array is nearly infinite, we will consider a specific example to better understand the process. To use this method in your program, you must perform the appropriate calculations to direct the pointers to the right place.

In Program 6.13 we want to move the elements of an array of integers, from M%(I) to M%(I + 1). Since the maximum number of integers that can be contained in a string is 127, the length of every string of the array A$ will be set to 254 (two bytes per integer). Figure 6.5 shows how the different elements of A$ and B$ are changed so that they point to the right location in the integer array.

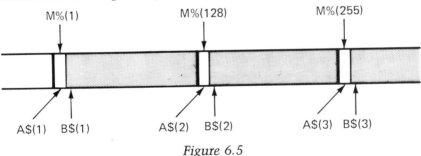

Figure 6.5

Since the actual copying of the string is performed character by character, using LSET directly to move every A$ to B$ would result in an error. (Why?) Thus, we use an intermediate string variable C$ to transfer A$ to B$.

```
10 ' ** Move part of array **
20 HOME
30 DEFINT A-Z:
   INPUT"Number of integers ";N:
```

```
     INPUT"Start moving at ";K
 35  DIM M(N):FOR I=1 TO N:M(I)=I:NEXT
 40  DEF FN MODULO(X!)=X!-256*INT(X!/256)
 50  X=0:Y=0:Z=0:L=0:A1!=0:A2!=0:
     AA!=0:AB!=0:I=0:W$="":J=0
 60  A$=SPACE$(254):B$=SPACE$(254):C$=SPACE$(254)
 70  X=VARPTR(A$):Y=VARPTR(B$):Z=VARPTR(C$):
     AA!=256*PEEK(X+2)+PEEK(X+1):AB!=256*PEEK(Y+2)+PEEK(Y+1)
 75  PRINT"Press <RETURN> to start ";:W$=INPUT$(1):PRINT
 80    FOR I=K TO N STEP 127
 85      PRINT CHR$(13);I;
 90      IF I+127<=N THEN L=254 ELSE L=(N-I+1)*2
100      A2!=VARPTR(M(I)):
         IF A2!<0
           THEN
             A2!=A2!+65536!
105      A1!=A2!+2
110      POKE X,L:POKE Y,L:POKE Z,L
120      POKE X+1,FN MODULO(A1!):POKE X+2,INT(A1!/256):
         POKE Y+1,FN MODULO(A2!):POKE Y+2,INT(A2!/256)
130      LSET C$=A$:LSET B$=C$:NEXT
140  FOR I=1 TO N:PRINT I" "M(I):NEXT
```

Program 6.13

6.2.9 MOVING RANGES OF MEMORY

There is no direct way to transfer a range of memory from one place to another in BASIC, yet sometimes it is not only convenient but necessary to do so. (A sequence of PEEK's and POKE's can be used, but the process is slow if the range is big.) An example of such a transfer is copying an entire screen when using mapped video (when the terminal shows the contents of some area of memory) or when you have a machine-language program in memory. Instead of POKEing number by number, you should be able to move the whole screen or program with a minimum of commands.

The same method used to move arrays can be applied here: if you make a string variable or string array point to the right locations, very simple LSET's or RSET's can move the range of memory into the location you want.

Let's look at an example. Suppose you have mapped video in your computer and want to store a particular screen for later use. If your display has 80*24 characters, you will need an array of eight string variables to store it. Setting the pointers to the right locations and using LSET, you can make a copy of the video memory. You can then change the screen, and whenever you want to bring the previous one back, you can use LSET again, this time with the video memory as destination. What once meant using many PRINT's can now be accomplished nearly instantly, the bigger the range to move, the greater the savings in time.

6.3 DISK BUFFER POINTERS

When used with a file number, the address returned by VARPTR (e.g., X = VARPTR(#2)) is the beginning of the disk buffer. In sequential files it is impossible to FIELD the buffer, so you cannot examine its contents before they are actually read by INPUT#'s. Using the address returned by VARPTR(#) to redirect a string variable to the buffer, however, you can study it before actually fetching the data.

6.3.1 DOING MASSIVE TRANSFERS TO DISK

When you want to do massive movements from memory to disk or vice versa, you can save much time by using the buffer as a regular string and doing the movement of arrays of numbers through strings. Using a buffer length of 128 bytes, Program 6.14 moves an array of 5000 integers by means of only forty disk transfers, compared with the 5000 usually required. The speeds of disk transfers vary considerably, but as a guide for comparison, our measurements showed that it took only 6.5 seconds to save the 5000 integers in an Apple II computer, and 13 seconds for 10,000 integers, as against 71 seconds for 5000 and 144 seconds for 10,000 in a regular sequential file. Since the arrays are read with the same technique, reading data from disk is at least as fast as, and usually faster than, transfering it as above.

```
10 '
                        ** MASSMOVE **
                Save 5000 integers with pointers.

20 OPTION BASE 1:N=5000:X=0:Y=0:Z=0:
   DIM M%(N),A$(40):
   FOR I%=1 TO N:
     M%(I%)=INT(1000*RND):
   NEXT:W$=""+"":FACTOR=2^16
25 DEF FN MODULO(X,Y)=X-INT(X/Y)*Y:
   DEF FN DIV(X,Y)=INT(X/Y)
30 OPEN"R",1,"DUMMY",128:FIELD 1,128 AS C$:
   Y=VARPTR(M%(1))
40 FOR I%=1 TO 39:
     Z=VARPTR(A$(I%)):POKE Z,128:
     X=VARPTR(M%((I%-1)*128+1)):
   IF X<0
     THEN
       X=X+FACTOR
```

```
45    POKE Z+1,FN MODULO(X,256):
      POKE Z+2,FN DIV(X,256):
   NEXT
50 I%=40:Z=VARPTR(A$(I%)):POKE Z,8:
   X=VARPTR(M%((I%-1)*128+1)):
   IF X<0
      THEN
         X=X+FACTOR
55    POKE Z+1,FN MODULO(X,256):
      POKE Z+2,FN DIV(X,256)
60 FOR I%=1 TO 40:
      LSET C$=A$(I%):PUT 1,I%:PRINT CHR$(13);I%;:
   NEXT
```

Program 6.14

Exercises

1. Write a program that will let you use a string as an array of 127 integers.

2. Write a version of the insertion sort using the technique described in Section 6.2.8 to move all the numbers and make room for the one to be inserted. If you combine this program with a binary search to look for the position of the new number, the program will re-sort the array so rapidly, that you will hardly notice the delay after entering the number. The program will be optimal for large arrays that must be read from the keyboard.

3. Write a set of subroutines to handle strings as if they did not have a length limit, using a numeric array to store the strings and the pointers of a string array to do the bookkeeping. Include the equivalent of the functions RIGHT$, LEFT$, and MID$.

4. The string descriptor blocks of an array are placed in consecutive locations (three bytes apart) beginning at the address returned by VARPTR of the first element of the array. Write a program to move the elements of an array of strings one place up (M$(I + 1) = M$(I), for example), considering the string descriptor blocks as a numeric array of a new type that uses three bytes per element.

UTILITIES

7

7.1 BINARY NUMBERS

The system of numbers we use in our everyday calculations is called the *decimal system*. Its name derives from the facts that every value is represented in groups of ten and ten digits (zero through nine) are used. Let's see how the position of every digit clearly defines its value. The number 703 actually means:

$$
\begin{array}{rcl}
7*100, & \text{or} & 7*10\wedge2 \\
+\ \ 0*\ 10, & \text{or} & 0*10\wedge1 \\
+\ \ 3*\ \ 1, & \text{or} & 3*10\wedge0
\end{array}
$$

The *binary system* uses only two digits, zero and one. It is important because computers represent everything internally—numbers, instructions, even characters and strings—with ones and zeros. At the present state of technology it is easier to work with only two different states (ON of OFF, LOW or HIGH, 0 or 1) than with ten.

In the binary system, the positions of the digits indicate different powers of two, just as in the decimal system we use powers of ten. The decimal number 703 would be represented as 1010111111 in binary. The conversion into decimal can be seen in Figure 7.1.

```
      1 * 512      (512 = 2^9)
 +    0 * 256      (256 = 2^8)
 +    1 * 128      (128 = 2^7)
 +    0 *  64      ( 64 = 2^6)
 +    1 *  32      ( 32 = 2^5)
 +    1 *  16      ( 16 = 2^4)
 +    1 *   8      (  8 = 2^3)
 +    1 *   4      (  4 = 2^2)
 +    1 *   2      (  2 = 2^1)
 +    1 *   1      (  1 = 2^0)
 ─────────────
Total = 703
```

Figure 7.1 Conversion from binary to decimal

To find the binary equivalent of a decimal number, perform successive integer divisions by powers of two, discarding the fractional part at each turn. Figure 7.2 shows the process of finding the binary equivalent of the decimal number 61.

```
61 DIV 128 = 0      61 −  0 = 61
61 DIV  64 = 0      61 −  0 = 61
61 DIV  32 = 1      61 − 32 = 29
29 DIV  16 = 1      29 − 16 = 13
13 DIV   8 = 1      13 −  8 =  5
 5 DIV   4 = 1       5 −  4 =  1
 1 DIV   2 = 0       1 −  0 =  1
 1 DIV   1 = 1       1 −  1 =  0
       61 in binary = 00111101
```

Figure 7.2 Conversion from decimal to binary

In microcomputers the basic unit of information is the *bit*, which can take one of two values: one or zero. To make things a little easier, bits are grouped into *bytes*, each byte comprising eight bits. When a byte has all its bits zero (00000000), its value is (decimal) 0; when all are ones, its value is 255. Therefore, a byte can be used to store any value between 0 and 255. A partial list of equivalences is given in Figure 7.3, where the peculiar pattern followed by these numbers is evident.

```
00000000 =  0      11110011 = 243
00000001 =  1      11110100 = 244
00000010 =  2      11110101 = 245
00000011 =  3      11110110 = 246
```

```
00000100 =  4        11110111 = 247
00000101 =  5        11111000 = 248
00000110 =  6        11111001 = 249
00000111 =  7        11111010 = 250
00001000 =  8        11111011 = 251
00001001 =  9        11111100 = 252
00001010 = 10        11111101 = 253
00001011 = 11        11111110 = 254
00001100 = 12        11111111 = 255
```

Figure 7.3 Binary and decimal equivalents

In BASIC there are four ways to work directly with bytes:

1. ASC: Returns the value (in decimal) of the argument.
2. CHR$: Returns the character that corresponds to the argument.
3. PEEK: Returns the contents of a certain byte in memory.
4. POKE: Puts a value in a memory location.

7.1.1 REPRESENTING NUMBERS GREATER THAN 255

Since a byte can only store numbers up to 255, the way to store larger numbers is to use two bytes, one of which is understood as multiplied by 256, allowing the representation of numbers from zero to 65,535, as shown in Figure 7.4.

First byte	Second byte	Equivalence
1	0	1 + 256* 0 = 1
255	0	255 + 256* 0 = 255
0	1	0 + 256* 1 = 256
1	1	1 + 256* 1 = 257
255	254	254 + 256*255 = 65534
255	255	255 + 256*255 = 65535

Figure 7.4 Two-byte representation

7.2 BOOLEAN VARIABLES

Besides the three standard numerical types (integer, single precision, and double precision) there is a fourth type that manages to remain hidden in most programs: the Boolean (or logical) type. Its peculiarity is that it can only take two values: TRUE or FALSE. The internal representations of these values are -1 and 0, respectively.[1] Since any of the three numerical types can store these two numbers, Boolean values can be stored in any numerical variable.

Boolean values are usually the result of comparisons or logical expressions. You are certainly familiar with instructions of the type

IF I>12 THEN. .

where the THEN part is executed only if the comparison is TRUE. That is exactly where a Boolean value is produced. Its occurrence is not so obvious, however, in the line

A = (I > 12):IF A THEN. .

The parentheses around the $I>12$ have been added to separate the Boolean expression from the assignment statement and are not essential. If $I=20$ in the first instruction, for example, the variable A gets TRUE (-1), and the IF A THEN branches to the THEN part.

7.2.1 LOGICAL OPERATORS

Boolean values have their own set of operations. When you execute an instruction of the type

IF (VALUE<300) AND (MONEY>1000) THEN . .

you are actually using one of the logical operations, which can be interpreted as 'if the first Boolean value is TRUE AND the second is also TRUE, THEN. .'. Definitions of all the Boolean operators are given in a truth table, which shows the results of all the possible combinations of the operands. Table 7.1 is the truth table for the AND operator.

A	B	A AND B
FALSE	FALSE	FALSE
FALSE	TRUE	FALSE
TRUE	FALSE	FALSE
TRUE	TRUE	TRUE

Table 7.1 Truth table for AND

From the truth table, we can derive that the only way for an AND operation to be TRUE is to have both operands TRUE; otherwise, the result is FALSE. Appendix B shows the truth tables for all six Boolean operators (AND, OR, NOT, XOR, IMP, and EQU).

---

[1] Any nonzero value is considered TRUE by BASIC; however, the result of comparisons is always 0 or -1.

7.2.2 LOGICAL OPERATIONS ON NON-BOOLEAN VALUES

The six Boolean operators can be used with standard integer values to execute logical operations at the bit level. Consider the following example:

A = 3   (in binary : 00000011)
B = 2   (in binary : 00000010)

A AND B = 2   (in binary : 00000010)

In the AND operation, every bit in A is compared with the corresponding bit in B. If both are ones, the resulting bit is one. (That is why the next-to-last bit of the result is a one); otherwise, the result is zero. The operation is a Boolean AND on every bit, in which the value 1 is considered TRUE and 0 FALSE.

In Table 7.2, the bytes with one bit ON are all powers of two:

$$
\begin{array}{rcrl}
00000001 &=& 1 & (2 \wedge 0) \\
00000010 &=& 2 & (2 \wedge 1) \\
00000100 &=& 4 & (2 \wedge 2) \\
00001000 &=& 8 & (2 \wedge 3) \\
00010000 &=& 16 & (2 \wedge 4) \\
00100000 &=& 32 & (2 \wedge 5) \\
01000000 &=& 64 & (2 \wedge 6) \\
10000000 &=& 128 & (2 \wedge 7)
\end{array}
$$

Table 7.2 Bytes with one bit ON

If you want to turn ON or OFF all the bits of a byte but one, a single operation is necessary:

N = 2   (N = 00000010)
N = NOT (N)   (N = 11111101)

An OR operation can turn a particular bit ON:

N = 0   (N = 00000000)
N = N OR 32   (00000000
               OR 00100000
                   00100000 = 32);

N = 109   (N = 01101101)
N = N OR 24   (01101101
               OR 00011000
                   01111101 = 125)

To check whether a particular bit is ON, AND the byte with a number in which all the bits are zero, except for the one you want to test:

```
N = 109          (N = 01101101
N = N AND 4      (    01101101
                     00000100
                 ─────────────
                     00000100 = 4);
```

If the result is different from zero, the bit is ON.

7.3 TAKING AWAY INDENTATIONS FROM PROGRAMS

As discussed in the Introduction, the characters added to program lines to make them more readable have two side effects: the programs are bigger (they need more space), and they run a little more slowly. This price is well worth the effort because the clarity of the programs can help you cut down the time to program and debug. However, if you must worry about every bit of space and time, program UNINDENT (Program 7.1) returns a program to its normal, unindented form. The process is very simple. A program that has been SAVEd in ASCII form (with the ,A option) is read into a string array in line 20. Lines 30 through 34 copy each line number in a parallel array LIN.NUM% and take out this number along with any nonsignificant characters (such as line-feed, tab, space) before the first instruction of every string, to facilitate the analysis. If the resulting line has at least one line-feed (which is where the indentations begin), line 90 calls subroutine 500 to delete all the nonsignificant characters after and including the line-feed. Subroutine 500 must consider two different cases: (1) if the character before the line-feed is a "`:`", then every nonsignificant character must be deleted; and (2) otherwise, the instruction is an IF, a THEN, or an ELSE, and a space must be left to avoid situations like "IF A = 12THEN30ELSE20".

Line 11 gives you the option of seeing or not seeing the program as it is generated. At the end of the process, the lines are reassembled with their numbers, and the entire program is SAVEd to disk once more.

Since the version with the indentations is much easier to understand, it is always a good idea to keep a copy of it and use the plain version to execute the program.

```
0 '
                            ** UNSTRUC **
                Take away indentations in program.

10 I=1:DIM PROGR$(100),LIN.NUM%(100):
   TAB$=CHR$(9):CTRL.J$=CHR$(10):TRUE=-1:
   FALSE=0:CR.RET$=CHR$(13)
11 HOME:
   INPUT"Show new program (DEFAULT:YES) ";TEMP$:
   IF TEMP$=""OR LEFT$("YES",LEN(TEMP$))=TEMP$
    THEN
       SHOW=TRUE
    ELSE
       SHOW=FALSE
15 DEF FN REMOVE$(X$,START,ENDING)=
   LEFT$(X$,START-1)+RIGHT$(X$,LEN(X$)-ENDING+1):
   DEF FN VL$(X)=RIGHT$(STR$(X),LEN(STR$(X))-1)
20 INPUT"FILENAME : ";FILE$:OPEN"I",1,FILE$:
   WHILE NOT EOF(1):
     LINE INPUT#1,PROGR$(I):I=I+1:
   WEND:
   CLOSE:N=I-1
30 FOR I=1 TO N
32    J=1:FOUND=FALSE:
   WHILE J<LEN(PROGR$(I)) AND NOT FOUND:
      TEMP$=MID$(PROGR$(I),J,1)
33      IF (TEMP$>="0" AND TEMP$<="9") OR TEMP$=" "
           OR TEMP$=TAB$ OR TEMP$=CTRL.J$
           OR TEMP$=CR.RET$
          THEN
            J=J+1
          ELSE
            FOUND=TRUE
34    WEND:
   LIN.NUM%(I)=VAL(PROGR$(I)):
   PROGR$(I)=RIGHT$(PROGR$(I),LEN(PROGR$(I))-J+1)
90    POSIT=INSTR(PROGR$(I),CTRL.J$):
   IF POSIT<>0
      THEN
         GOSUB 500:GOTO 90
100    PROGR$(I)=FN VL$(LIN.NUM%(I))+" "+PROGR$(I):
   IF SHOW
      THEN
         PRINT PROGR$(I)
110 NEXT
120 PRINT:
   PRINT"Name to save new program ";:
   PRINT " (DEFAULT:"FILE$") ";:
   INPUT SAVE.FILE$:
   IF SAVE.FILE$<>""
      THEN
         FILE$=SAVE.FILE$
```

```
130 OPEN"O",1,FILE$:
    FOR I%=1 TO N:
      PRINT#1,PROGR$(I%):
    NEXT:CLOSE:END
499 END

500 '
   ** Subroutine DELETE UNTIL NEXT CHARACTER **

505 IF POSIT<>1
    THEN
      IF MID$(PROGR$(I),POSIT-1,1)<>":"
        THEN
          MID$(PROGR$(I),POSIT,1)=" ":
          POSIT=POSIT+1
510 J=POSIT+1:FOUND=FALSE:
    WHILE J<=LEN(PROGR$(I)) AND NOT FOUND:
      TEMP$=MID$(PROGR$(I),J,1):
      IF TEMP$<>" "AND TEMP$<>CTRL.J$
        AND TEMP$<>TAB$ AND TEMP$<>CR.RET$
        THEN
          FOUND=TRUE
        ELSE
          J=J+1
520 WEND:
    IF FOUND
      THEN
        PROGR$(I)=FN REMOVE$(PROGR$(I),POSIT,J)
530 RETURN
```

Program 7.1

APPENDICES

ASCII CODE

A

0	Null	19	Device control 3	38	&
1		20	Device control 4	39	'
2		21		40	(
3		22		41	)
4		23		42	*
5		24	Cancel	43	+
6		25		44	,
7	Bell	26		45	–
8	Backspace	27	Escape	46	.
9	Tab	28		47	/
10	Line-feed	29		48	0
11	Vertical tab	30		49	1
12	Form-feed	31		50	2
13	Carriage return	32	Space	51	3
14	Shift out	33	!	52	4
15	Shift in	34	"	53	5
16		35	#	54	6
17	Device control 1	36	$	55	7
18	Device control 2	37	%	56	8

57	9	81	Q	105	i
58	:	82	R	106	j
59	;	83	S	107	k
60	<	84	T	108	l
61	=	85	U	109	m
62	>	86	V	110	n
63	?	87	W	111	o
64	@	88	X	112	p
65	A	89	Y	113	q
66	B	90	Z	114	r
67	C	91	[	115	s
68	D	92	\	116	t
69	E	93	]	117	u
70	F	94	∧	118	v
71	G	95	_	119	w
72	H	96	'	120	x
73	I	97	a	121	y
74	J	98	b	122	z
75	K	99	c	123	{
76	L	100	d	124	¦
77	M	101	e	125	}
78	N	102	f	126	~
79	O	103	g	127	Delete
80	P	104	h		

TRUTH TABLES
OF THE LOGICAL OPERATORS
B

AND:

A	B	A AND B
FALSE	FALSE	FALSE
FALSE	TRUE	FALSE
TRUE	FALSE	FALSE
TRUE	TRUE	TRUE

OR:

A	B	A OR B
FALSE	FALSE	FALSE
FALSE	TRUE	TRUE
TRUE	FALSE	TRUE
TRUE	TRUE	TRUE

NOT:

A	NOT A
FALSE	TRUE
TRUE	FALSE

XOR:

A	B	A XOR B
FALSE	FALSE	FALSE
FALSE	TRUE	TRUE
TRUE	FALSE	TRUE
TRUE	TRUE	FALSE

IMP:

A	B	A IMP B
FALSE	FALSE	TRUE
FALSE	TRUE	TRUE
TRUE	FALSE	FALSE
TRUE	TRUE	TRUE

EQU:

A	B	A EQU B
FALSE	FALSE	TRUE
FALSE	TRUE	FALSE
TRUE	FALSE	FALSE
TRUE	TRUE	TRUE

INDEX

A

AND 142, 143, 151
Array 97, 102, 123, 124, 132, 135
ASCII 2, 32, 111, 149

B

Batch 38
Binary
  Numbers 139
  Search 66
Bit 118, 140
Boolean
  Functions 109
  Variables 118, 141, 143
Buffer 90, 92, 93, 95, 137
Buffering 90
Byte 93, 94, 117, 118, 140

C

Case 32, 66
Commands, predefined 41
Control Characters 2, 52, 103, 130
Cursor 3, 21
CVD, CVI, CVS 95, 126, 128, 133

I

L

M

N